Down and Out

The Collected Writings of
The Oldie columnist

Wilfred De'Ath

Illustrations by Larry

with an introduction by
Melvyn Bragg

ANDRE
DEUTSCH

First published in 2003 by
André Deutsch Ltd
An imprint of the
Carlton Publishing Group
20 Mortimer Street
London W1T 3JW

A catalogue record for this book is available
from the British Library

ISBN 0 233 00056 9

Printed in Great Britain
by Mackays

Contents

Introduction

by Melvyn Bragg

I've known Wilfred for more than 40 years. I don't think we met each other at Oxford though we were contemporaries. My first clear memory of meeting him is outside a lift in Broadcasting House. He struck me then as extremely mild mannered, ready with a giggle, a floppy haired bohemian, and perhaps a little like a French Dancing Master – and if I did think the latter at the time then it was prophetic given the way he has led the French a dance.

I was pleased to encounter a genial, charming literary man who felt as lucky to be working for BBC Radio as I did. That was near the beginning of the 60s. He married and our wives knew each other a little. He wrote book reviews for the Times and may well have written elsewhere for all I know. He was putting a life together as a broadcaster and journalist, good for a steady BBC career, ready for a column, tipped for a book or two. He was one of that friendly outer circle of peer group acquaintances who make you feel you might be part of a generation, even a purposeful generation.

We met irregularly but I never saw the least sign of whatever it was that turned him into "a criminal and a scrounger" (copyright *The Oldie*), a down and out, a sort of wan, ghostly, anglicised Genet, or a figure out of Evelyn Waugh, fortune felled by fate. And now? Well he is a columnist, probably soon to go back as a broadcaster, he has a book coming out and he has been sustained in his writing by another Oxford contemporary Richard Ingrams.

What happened in between? I've never asked. In fact I haven't seen him for about 20 years although we correspond regularly. There are mutterings on the domestic wire but they never made sentences. He has probably had the most curious life of anyone of my Oxford generation. Banged up with tattooed murderers, sharing cells with drug addicts, living off prostitutes, chucked out of religious retreats despite his persistent religion, and even stealing from a candle box. His mild exposure and idiosyncratic testing of official Christian charity is one of his rare forays into a sustained social comment.

Mostly he's just blown along by the wind. Now he lands on his feet – which means a good meal, good wine, neither of which he can afford, bed and books. On the next page he inhabits a hell of menace, rave music, double handcuffs, claustrophobia and humiliation. The odd thing is that neither seem to touch him very much.

Whatever it is, it gets another column, over crammed with incidents and characters, thrown away, so much material passing through his life, material that most of his contemporaries "would die for" (a favourite phrase of his).

Then I get yet another charming, scrounging letter on graph paper torn from an exercise book which he may have pinched in the sixth form, saying that he is starving to death (literally), about to be ejected even from the gutter, banged up again – there is nothing tentative, reticent or Old English about Wilfred's description of his condition when he wants cash.

It's difficult to keep remembering that Wilfred really has done some bad things. For a start, people who run small hotels will go bust if their clients walk out without paying. Then there is the fantasy – or is it? – the claim that wherever he goes in France women are on fire for his loins? Then he takes a seven year vow of chastity. Of course. Is he a holy fool? Is he anybody's fool? Is he one of the "pure in heart?" or have circumstances propelled him into a universe of his own where the only possible life he can lead is indeed a life blown on the wind?

Confessions of an Oldie Lag

I was sent to prison for the first time in 1990 at the age of 53. Since then I have been inside half-a-dozen times, normally on remand, but once as a convicted prisoner in HMP Exeter. (I have also done porridge in Oxford and Winchester.) My offence has always been the same: obtaining services by deception, which in my case means staying at an hotel and not paying the bill.

As an oldie, I have generally been treated well by staff and other inmates. This is no less to do with my age than the fact that prisons are, contrary to myth, extremely polite places. Everyone treats everyone else with great respect because, basically, they are rather frightened of you. After all, until you choose to tell them, they don't know what you are in for. It might be for murder or it might be for not paying your TV licence. When I reveal that I am in there for fraud, my cell mates look rather disappointed. Possibly they were hoping to be banged up with a serial sex-killer or something. (In that case, I would ask to be put under Rule 43 for my own protection.)

The one time I was not treated well in jail was on admission to HMP Exeter in 1993 when I stupidly told the landing tea-orderly, who by long prison tradition allots cells to new arrivals, that I was an 'intellectual' and wanted a cell by myself. This was a fatal mistake, since every kind of education is regarded with derision in prison. Word spread like wildfire and people came from all over the jail to spit upon me. The 'tea-boat' orderly, a drugs smuggler who was reaching the end of a hefty stretch, literally spat into my cell every time he passed it (twice a day, delivering tea) until he left. Later, 'on the out,' I ran into him in a pub and he was perfectly civil, having no need to maintain the machismo contempt for intellectuals. For one awful moment I thought he was going to buy me a drink.

I should add that I got very fed up with being spat upon twice a day and, at one point, made a rather feeble complaint to an officer. He hid behind my cell door, watched the spittle fly through the air, and then proposed to do absolutely nothing about it: 'You get that type in prison,' was his laconic, unhelpful comment. As a generalisation, I would say that prison officers are even more degraded – and certainly use worse language – than the men they are paid to look after. Some of the younger ones are not too bad, having been trained in more humane methods, but I genuinely believe that the older ones go home and lock up their wives in the kitchen. There was a certain Mr Hunt (I expect you can imagine his nickname) who gave me a particularly bad time because I declined to shave every day (I have a very light beard). Growing a beard in prison is a serious offence because it means you must be planning to escape in disguise.

There are a number of myths about prison life and I should like to explode a few of them. The first is that time passes slowly. It doesn't. The structure of the regime (lunch at 11, supper at 4, locked up for the night at 5 or 6) means that each day is a short one, so that a week passes very quickly indeed. This is true even of a relatively long sentence. Before you know it, you are back 'on the out' again and wondering how to turn an honest penny.

The second myth is that prison food is bad. It isn't. A cell mate of mine once called it 'airline food' and I think that is a good description though, admittedly, it is not an airline I should wish to fly with. Some of the meals are not bad. Breakfast is particularly appetising if you can stomach it after a long night: (porridge in winter), bacon and egg, as much tea, toast, butter and marmalade

2

as you can manage. I never had a good meal in prison, but I never had a really bad one.

Third myth: they lock you up for 23 hours a day. Not true, except in very dire emergencies. You are normally allowed out about five or six hours a day and you can get plenty of exercise – either just walking along the landings or in the yard. (As chaplain's orderly in Exeter, I was allowed the run of the whole prison, including the Rule 43s – sex offenders – and I was never confined to my cell.)

Fourth myth: prisons are hopelessly overcrowded and you are 'banged up' two, three and four to a cell. Again, not true in my experience. In fact, I have only ever had three cell-mates at various times: one a young tearaway who regularly beat me at chess; one a pathetic alcoholic; the third an aggressive Scotsman, in for 'unlawful wounding', who was quite a nice chap when you got to know him. Most of the time, I have been given a cell to myself, doubtless because I am (dread word) an 'intellectual' and an oldie at that. I am a great user of prison libraries, which are excellent (as you can order books from the outside). I average 15 books a week while behind bars.

Biggest myth of all: prisons are understaffed. They are not. I counted 17 officers around the hot-plate at breakfast at HMP Winchester last time I was there. (Admittedly, it was winter-time). They are all on about £25,000 a year. (Their union likes to propagate the myth that prisons are understaffed.)

I am frequently asked by less literate prisoners to help them write sexy letters home to their wives and girlfriends (no easy task) and, more importantly, for those on remand, to help them prepare their pleas in mitigation for when they go to court. A very young, charming, armed robber (first offence) asked me what I thought he might get. Judging it by a similar case I knew, I rashly said 'probation'. He got seven-and-a-half years. I guess he was unlucky with the judge. I was rather concerned that he might kill me, but he was very pleasant and philosophical when he came back from court.

Perhaps I have given the impression that I don't mind being in prison. That would, to some extent, be true (the worst part about being caught up in the criminal justice system is having to hang around magistrates' courts – truly depressing places), although I don't think I could handle a very long sentence. The most I have done is four months, 'a shit and a shave,' as they say. British prisons are a curious mixture of public school, the army and a lunatic asylum – the latter ingredient in particular. Most of the people held in them are pathetic and inadequate and should never have been sent there.

I expect to go back soon (HMP Dorchester this time) and, while it would not be true to say that I am looking forward to it, I really don't mind very much. I feel quite safe in prison. And one's creditors cannot get at one.

Vive la Freebies!

English friends do not believe that I have lived in France for five years without any money. I fell into this way of life by chance in 1992, when, arrested for not paying a hotel bill in Caen, I was dragged, handcuffed, in front of the Procureur de la Republique (State Prosecutor) who, after commenting sarcastically, 'I suppose even in England – *même en Angleterre* – people usually settle their hotel bills,' ordered the gendarmes to release me to an *asile de nuit* or night shelter.

This was not the most pleasant of places, full of drunks, tramps and neurotics, but it set me on the path which, apart from a few brief intervals in England under legal restraint, I am still treading today. I spent six pretty uncomfortable nights in the *asile*, though the spaghetti they served at supper was the best I have ever tasted. In Angers, three weeks later, in trouble again, I was directed to the Abri de la Providence (literally, providential shelter) where, on my first night, an elderly German resident told me that we had the good fortune to be staying at the equivalent of a two-star family hotel. This turned out to be true. I stayed for three months.

For 15 francs (about £1.50), which you paid only if you could afford it, you were given a comfortable bed and a superb, nourishing meal: soup, salad, boiled beef and carrots, cheese, yoghurt and fruit was a typical menu. The ambience was distinctly familial and the humane director, very pro-British, encouraged me to sing for my supper (since I couldn't pay) - by giving English lessons to staff and residents, which I did once a week.

The inmates of Abri de la Providence were a pretty mixed lot – not so much tramps and drunks (though there were a few of those) as middle-class men who had simply fallen on hard times – deserted by their wives, lost their jobs and had their houses repossessed. They were excellent company, and taught me to speak good French. To a large extent, I identified with them. For several weeks, at supper, I sat next to a former member of Pompidou's government – I didn't believe him at first until he conducted me to the Angers Library and proudly showed me a photo of his younger self seated at a table with Pompidou and de Gaulle during the *événements* of 1968.

Even in Angers, however, I knew that *foyer*-wise (foyer means 'home' or 'hostel') better things lay ahead. One heard talk of a terrestrial paradise, a *foyer de luxe* named Antipoul which is situated in the great south-west city of Toulouse. I made it there in February 1993 – I travel free on SNCF – and have lived there, on and off, ever since. For a mere five francs a night – which, again, you don't have to pay if you haven't got it – you share an austere but comfortable and extremely clean room with one other SDF (*Sans Domicile Fixe* or No Fixed Abode) like yourself. This is, admittedly, a bit of a lottery. I have stayed with filthy Arabs, with drunks, tramps, drug addicts, and university professors down on their luck. I am quite ruthless about getting rid of any *voisin* (room-mate) who troubles me too much. I simply complain to the director. As long as the *voisin* doesn't smoke in the room (forbidden anyway) or snore too loudly, then I am content. At present, I am sharing with a Spanish workman who is impeccable, and, as they say, extremely *sage* (well-behaved).

Breakfast is buffet-style from 6.30am and consists of exactly what you would be served in a three- or four-star French hotel: café au lait or chocolate, fresh bread, butter and jam. You have to be out during the day for your room to be cleaned (you lunch free at the magnificent, futuristic Restaurant Social, shaped like a flying saucer) then go back again at five for a shower and a shave and –

here we get to the nub – the meal of your gastronomic dreams.

I once read in a food guide that the sign of a really good meal is that you leave the table not merely satisfied but exhilarated and Antipoul does that for me night after night. Take last night, more or less at random. It happened to be my 60th birthday, which I had spent in Lourdes – two hours away by train – so I was quite tired and hungry when I got back to the *foyer* at 9pm. The staff served soup, a carrot-based salad, two bowls of spaghetti and two fresh melons – a birthday feast, but nothing special by Antipoul standards.

There are *foyers* in France (every large city has one) where you eat even better than this. In Avignon, a hospital dating from the First World War and once run by the Franciscan Friars has been taken over by the (extremely rich) town and is now another *foyer de luxe* for the SDF. No one will believe that for a mere 20 francs (again, you pay only in you can afford it) you are given as much quality Norwegian smoked salmon as you can eat. This is normally preceded by a fine soup, full of pasta, followed by, say, roast chicken on rice salad, Camembert, yoghurt and fruit. The young pro-British director, Roland, has a thing about writers and says it is an honour to have me there. I reply that the honour is all mine.

Limoges is not my favourite French city – rather a grey place – but at 45 Avenue Emile-Labussiere is another *foyer* where I have made friends for life. Michel, the director, an ex-boxer, protects me from the (frequently expressed) anti-British sentiments of the other residents. He is like a brother to me. Françoise, the waitress, cries when I arrive and cries again when I leave – I send her postcards from England, when on remand, which I truly believe she will keep by her bedside until the day she dies. These people offer a warmth and hospitality which I have not encountered under any circumstances in England.

In La Rochelle, at the Foyer des Cordeliers, they ask you, horror of horrors, to do a daily task. So I do not stay there very long – a week at the most – although the food, served by nuns, is excellent. In La Roche-sur-Yon (almost the perfect French provincial town), at La Halte Foyer, everyone has to pitch in with the cleaning. So I do not stay there for very long either – five days at the most. Again, the *foyer* is superb.

What a selfish, self-indulgent bastard! My daughter, who has priggish tendencies, considers that, since I am living for nothing off the French state, I ought to be paying French *impots* or income tax. But how can I do that without a French income? (It is true that the French are very highly taxed in order to pay for all this.) I suppose that I feel the world owes me a living. As the possessor of an EC passport and with no means, I am perfectly entitled to stay at these *foyers*. So is anybody else in my situation. So the world is paying its debt to me. I wish I could say that I felt guilty about all this and that I agree with my daughter, but I don't. I repeat: anyone in possession of an EC passport and with no money is entitled to stay, for as long as they wish, at the French *foyer* – and without payment. Vive la France!

Confessions of a Catholic Scrounger

Recently I decided to make a short Catholic retreat, and it was arranged that I should spend a day or two with the sisters of Jeanne Delanoue, Mother of the Poor, at their *maison mère* in St Hilaire-St Florent, just outside Saumur. After about four days I felt so much better than I had for the first time in 20 years of retreat-going. I felt like leaving the good sisters some money. I didn't, of course, because I didn't have any, and anyway they didn't expect it, but the thought was there, at least.

In 1978, I spent an entire month with the Community of the Resurrection in Mirfield, Yorkshire, trying to decide whether or not to become a Roman Catholic (Mirfield, in fact, is very High Anglican). They had a guest-master who, far from making his guests feel welcome, always seemed glad to see the back of them. I shall never forget the look of smug satisfaction on his face as the taxi swept a departing guest away. This increased as he examined the large cheque the guest had left behind. I resolved to pay as little as possible for my stay and, in fact, gave him only £20 for the whole month. For many years after that Father Luke wrote to me regularly saying that I should 'not lose sight of' the money I still owed them.

I have always understood the principle of monastic hospitality to be that you treat your guest as though he were Jesus Christ come to stay for a while, and you certainly wouldn't dream of shoving a bill on Our Blessed Lord's breakfast plate within a few days of his arrival. But that is what increasingly happens in convents and monasteries these days.

They did try to maintain the monastic principle at Douai Abbey (Benedictines) where I often used to go on retreat after becoming RC. They never seemed to ask for, or expect, any money, so I would occasionally drop a fiver into the collection plate at Mass on Sunday, if I could afford it – or even if I couldn't. But even Douai, the most tolerant of places, got fed up with my freeloading. The Prior, who disliked me, caught me making a long-distance phone call to France and I became persona non grata after that. I understood why, of course, but I still maintain that in the strictest sense they were wrong to exclude me from their peaceful, religious life.

I used to go to Worth Abbey (also Benedictines) after that, where the Abbot put a full bottle of Scotch on the table of an evening and proclaimed that neither of us would make a move towards bed until it was empty. Neither of us did. Then I went to the snobbish Downside where the double-barrelled Bursar (I believe he is now Abbot) tried to institute criminal proceedings against me for bouncing a cheque on their bookshop. Downside is one of the richest monasteries in the world, presiding over 500 acres of rich farmland and an extremely expensive public school, they eat eight courses at dinner on Feast Days, yet they seem unable to accommodate a poor NFA (No Fixed Abode) like me even for a few days.

For some years I became the scourge of retreat houses all over England, leaving a trail of distraught guest-masters behind me. The Prior at Boar's Hill, Oxford (discalced Carmelites) still has a nervous breakdown when my name is mentioned, since I found a way of sneaking in to stay at the Priory for days at a time without informing anyone of my presence. I think they got angry because my presence in their midst underlined the essential hypocrisy of their position in respect of hospitality, which was epitomised for me (at Douai, I'm afraid) when we sang the psalm, 'And let me never forget my poorer brother' at midday office, and then watched the Prior see off a group of tramps who had gathered at the refectory door in search of nourishment. I suppose my own behaviour was a kind of tacit revenge, a way of saying that you can't have it both ways.

The only retreat house in the UK where I am still persona grata is, oddly, not a Catholic one at all, but a charismatic one, Fursey House in the New Forest, where they let me stay for several weeks without payment as recently as 1996. Money was never mentioned so, of course, I felt like paying. (But did you? No.)

Things are not much better here in France where I have been 'retreating' since 1991. The first retreat I ever went on was with some very weird nuns at a place called Beaufort, in a remote part of Brittany. Their liturgy included dancing around the altar at vespers and strange incantations at compline. It was all a shade eerie. I left them 200 francs, all I had on me, but the Prioress, who was a cripple, stamped her club-foot with rage and threatened me with the police. I don't think I shall be going back.

In 1992, I went to Solesmes, the great Benedictine Abbey in the Somme (160 monks), where the Abbot washes the hands and feet of each guest on his first evening. He welcomed me as 'an old Oxfordian' and said I might stay as long as I wished. I would have done so except that the *vin de table* they served at dinner tasted like red ink and gave me an upset stomach. I went back in 1994 but they had got wise to me by then and, after a few days, demanded *un petit cadeau*, ie money (precisely the term used by prostitutes in France). Also, the assistant guest-master, an American, was a raving queer who wouldn't stop dropping in to see me to discuss the state of my soul. So I got fed up and left. But I miss all those monks doing their Gregorian chant.

In Lourdes I stayed with the nuns at St Joseph's Convent. While I was there, someone broke in and desecrated their chapel and stole 2,000 francs. I was the suspect, so the nuns called in a Clouseau-like inspector who threatened to throw me into a bare cell, strip me naked and 'beat the living shit' out of me. In the end, he had to let me go for lack of evidence.

In October 1995, I stayed for a week at the famous Taizé Community in Burgundy. I slept in a broken bed in a room with no light bulb or washing facilities, sharing with an elderly German. We ate disgusting food in a broken-down tent, like refugees in a war zone. For this they wanted £100 a week! When I complained to Frère Roger, aged 82, a friend of the Pope and of the late Mother Teresa, he seemed quite startled. 'No one has ever complained before,' he said. 'You do not understand our difficulties here.' I understood them only too well. Their difficulty is getting gullible guests to pay through the nose to live in conditions you wouldn't keep a dog in. And all in the name of Christianity. Taizé was a kind of Christian concentration camp, where you were refused a cup of cold water.

I've only once, in 20 years, felt guilty about not paying for a retreat, and that was when I stayed with some Spanish sisters in Lourdes in December 1992. They really did seem poor, and I think they genuinely needed money. They belonged to an order called Sisters of the Love of God and, as I pointed out to their superior, that very title implied – to me, at any rate – that they must occasionally accommodate someone like myself for nothing. She seemed to see my point and, when she did so, I at once felt like paying her. And one day I shall.

Hotel of the
Living Dead

I thought the Belsize was an hotel like any other when I booked in there after being released from prison in 1996. I only learned later that they advertised themselves as the only above-ground cemetery in Eastbourne. I should have twigged this from the fact that the man who had booked in just before me, a gruff Yorkshireman named John Rhodes, was 92, my senior by 34 years.

Ninety-two he may have been, but Mr Rhodes still enjoyed his food ('The grub 'ere fair melts in yer mouth,' he told me on his first day) and drink (two large gins and tonic before dinner), and had an eye for the girls, particularly the 'Social, Welsh and Sexy' weather-girl Sian Lloyd on ITV – 'Glamour Puss,' he called her. In the hotel, no female, from 80-year-old pensioners down to the 16-year-old waitress, Angela, was safe while Mr Rhodes was around. He became my best friend at the Belsize. In fact, he was my only friend. Alas, he is no longer with us.

The Belsize specialised in elderly people who liked to believe that they still had private incomes but who – apart from one wealthy 82-year-old hypochondriac, Vera – actually lived on social security. Vera's family lived nearby (next door, actually), but had understandably shoved her, her maid, her private nurse, her hairdresser and her dog-walker (I do not exaggerate) to where she could lord and lady it over others and not themselves. Vera took a fancy to me for some horrible reason: 'Most of the people here live off the state, Wilfred,' she whispered to me one evening after dinner. 'Really, Vera?' I said, nervously, fingering the unemployment card in my inside pocket. Terence Rattigan would have rejected Vera as hopelessly over the top as a character for *Separate Tables*, his famous play about lonely people in a seaside hotel.

Separate tables was the name of the game at mealtimes when we all sat in our regular corners in the dining-room and glared at each other. The food was OK, if you liked Brown Windsor soup six nights out of seven. There was the Major to whom something unspeakable had happened during the war with Japan – whenever a 'Nip' appeared on the telly he used to get up and run to his room. I felt sorry for him, but not for the Captain (ex-US Army) who had come over with the first wave of American troops circa 1942 and never returned. Rumour held that the most action he had ever seen was on the sofa in the residents' lounge, but he had a fat US Army pension and used to order drinks before, with and after meals, so the proprietors fawned on him.

There was a classic English eccentric named Mr Woodhead, 82, who, at tea on my first afternoon, asked me how long I had been there. I said, 'About two hours,' and asked him how long *he* had been there. 'Twenty-eight years,' was his reply. Downwind Mr Woodhead gave off a truly revolting smell and he had a lump the size of a cricket ball just below his left ear. When I got to know Mr Woodhead, who wore a straw hat winter and summer, indoors and out, I cruelly asked him why he didn't have this operated on. 'What and lose my "lump" sum on retirement?' he quipped.

Most of the old ladies were alcoholics. Joan, whose three husbands had all committed suicide, drank vodka and watched cricket on the telly all day long – she was an avid Sussex fan. Mrs Edwards, a South African, had written the novel to end novels but never managed to get it published. Joyce was ashamed when I opened the hotel door to her psychiatric nurse. I failed to see why because she was no madder than the rest of them. A small, red-haired woman farted loudly whenever she got up from her chair and tried to cover it up with a cough. Worst of all was the woman who pushed her shopping trolley around the hotel corridors all night in order to be the first in the queue at Tesco next morning. She went there for the company, she told me.

Broadly speaking, the men were nicer than the women and better at dealing with old age. There was a nice old chap called Tim who used to invite me into his room to watch telly, but the smell of excrement and urine soon drove me out His friend, Ron, an avid supporter of Watford FC, also invited me in to watch football, but again, the urine smell drove me to make excuses. In the end, I took to going to the chemist's to pick up prescriptions for the pair of them; it got me out of the place for a while and away from the awful smell.

Quite a few people died during the three months I was at the Belsize. The proprietors seemed to regard death as something shameful, reflecting badly on their hotel. They used to pop the bodies into the garden shed during the night for removal by the undertakers the next morning, during breakfast, to avoid upsetting the other guests. No one was fooled.

Among 40 or so guests, I was one of the few who didn't use the chairlift. There was one younger than myself, Barry, in his 40s, a dead ringer for the Rowan Atkinson character Mr Bean, who had come to Easthourne to commit suicide by jumping off Beachy Head but somehow or other ended up in this House of the Living Dead – a poor alternative, one might think. He resented my going to the chemist to pick up prescriptions for Tim and Ron because, until my arrival, he had been the self-appointed male nurse of the establishment. The proprietors, in their turn, resented Barry because they liked to feel that they were in charge of medical matters. Wealthy Vera had already remembered them in her will. I couldn't help being reminded of Dr John Bodkin Adams who, in the 1950s, had 'eased the passing' of so many rich, elderly ladies in Eastbourne, where time has stood still.

There was something faintly sinister about Barry, but he had a good sense of humour and told really filthy stories, quite unprintable here. (I thought he might have a future as an alternative comedian.) This conflicted oddly with his devotion to a small group of biblical bigots in the hotel who used to hold prayer meetings in each other's bedrooms. I overheard them praying for *me* once. Then they went back to gossip, conjecturing as to whether or not I might have served a bit of 'time'. (I would quite gladly have told them had they bothered to ask.)

In the end, I got myself out of the Belsize by the simple expedient of not paying the bill. A year later, almost to the day, I ran into Barry Bean in the High Street. He was still there and broke: 'Can't even afford the bus fare up to Beachy Head,' he observed wryly – but almost everyone else had died. Two of the bigots had left and were living together as man and wife – occasionally they walked the seafront hand-in-hand. It's a funny old world.

Scrounger on the Run

This was a hard trip. It kicked off in Saumur, where, in late March, the weather was more like January. From school history I vaguely recall that Bismarck proudly described his Prussia as an army containing a state; well, Saumur, HQ of the French cavalry, is a barrack containing a town. Sitting in a bar tabac one morning, I watched an exquisitely accoutred French cavalry colonel and his ditto wife ride by on two well-manicured Normandy cobs. '*Voila mes impots*' – there go my taxes – said a gloomy man at the next table.

The Foyer des Quatre Saisons – the local free hostel for the homeless – lies in the shadow of Saumur castle, in a better position than the three-star hotel. The staff are, even by French *foyer* standards, exceptionally kind and caring. I went down with a bad dental abscess while I was there and they showered me with antibiotics and painkillers and found me the best dentist in town. All for free, of course. René, *le directeur*, could not have been more concerned: '*La porte est toujours ouverte*' – the door is always open – he told me on the day I left, having tried hard to persuade me to stay. But I knew in my heart that I would never return.

I took the train to Nantes. (The SNCF lets me travel free on production of my EC passport.) In La Roche-Sur-Yon, out on the Atlantic coast, at La Halte *foyer*, they expect you – *quel horreur* – to join in with the cleaning and washing up. So I was there for only three days before Christian, the director, who had once been my friend, threw me out as a scrounging Englishman. Well, fair enough. He was convinced that I was a rich tourist posing as an

SDF, whereas, as everyone now knows, I have not a sou in the whole wide world. The trouble is, I *look* well-off.

I took another train down to Saintes, then a bus to Angouleme, on which I managed to leave my reading specs – *un veritable catastrophe* for someone who reads as much as I do. Then yet another little train cross-country to Limoges, where it rained for 12 days *sans cesse*. Aida, the *foyer* tart, learning that I had no money, took pity on me and slipped off to the station, returning later with a fistful of 200-franc notes, of which she gave me several. This was not the first time in my life I had lived off the earnings of prostitutes, and I wish I could say it would be the last. The rain showed no sign of letting up, so I said *au revoir* to Aida and my other foyer friends and headed for the Pyrenees.

A friend once described me as a 'person to whom things happen'. This proved true in Tarbes, in the foothills of the Pyrenees, where Angelo, an ex-Legionnaire (he'd been fired from the Foreign Legion for being too violent, if you can imagine such a thing) went berserk in the *foyer* after a row over the washing-up and let off several rounds from the FL pistol he shouldn't have been carrying A bullet grazed my stomach and, for the third time in my life, I experienced that weird sensation of seeing my admittedly chequered past life flash before my eyes The French police now want me to appear as a witness at Angelo's trial but they can only get me while I'm in France, which is why I've come back to Britain where I'm wanted for other reasons*. I went on to Toulouse and the great *foyer-de-luxe*, Antipoul, but even here my previous good luck seemed to have run out. At Mass one morning in the local parish church, Sacré Coeur, I was foolish enough to leave my paltry worldly goods in the *vestiaire* (cloakroom) and a light-fingered Arab made off with them, leaving me with only the clothes I stood up in. The three priests on duty could not have been less helpful, they wouldn't even let me use their phone to ring the police. Not that I wanted to ring the police. I took the train to Avignon instead.

But Avignon was crawling with soldiers and police for the Chirac-Kohl summit, so it didn't seem wise to linger there either. It looked as though my good luck in France had finally run out. I left with some regret because at the Visa *foyer* I am always made very welcome (as described in *Oldie* 103), and one lives and eats like a king – as much quality Norwegian smoked salmon as you can manage.

So it was the TGV up to Paris (free again), my last 10-franc piece on the Metro Gare de Lyon, another free ride up to Cherbourg and then the ferry to Poole, after spending the night at the ferry port. I've had a good run in the free French *foyers* – nearly six years – and, like Edith Piaf, *je ne regrette rien*.

Merci et Vive la France!*

* De'Ath was not at at large for long.

Ship of De'Ath

On 18 May, in Dorchester, I was imprisoned for six months by the local magistrates for making off without payment from two hotels and for failing to attend an earlier hearing at their court. I was transported in handcuffs to the nearby Dorchester jail, a crumbling Victorian edifice built to house 200 prisoners. It now holds nearly twice that number in conditions of noise, stench and squalor. I spent three miserable weeks there, sharing a tiny cell with an extremely disturbed heroin addict (and dealer) who was going through 'cold turkey'.

Early in June, a senior 'screw' entered our cell and offered us both a choice of transfer to either HMP Dartmoor, or HMP Weare, the new 'floating prison' in Portland harbour (motto: Who Swims Wins!). We both, with alacrity, chose the boat. Originally built for oil-rig workers, then used to transport troops during the Falklands War (quite a few of the 'screws' had made that trip as servicemen), it was eventually sold as scrap to the Americans for £10,000. The Yanks sold it back for £5 million and another £9 million was spent on refurbishing it as a prison. £14 million! (Although to build a brand new prison would cost £60 million.)

On a bleak, rainy Monday morning, heavily chained and double-handcuffed, we were driven the short distance from Dorchester to Portland. Our spirits sank down to our prison-issue trainers as the grey steel hulk loomed over us in the mist. It looked like Auschwitz-on-Sea. Furthermore, the reception screws seemed to have, in prison parlance, 'a bad attitude' towards us. We were kept for several hours in a claustrophobic holding cell before being conducted to the B2 'Induction' deck. Suddenly, life was transformed. I was shown to a large single cabin with a sea view. There was an en suite lavatory and shower, carpet, all kinds of furniture and a selection of toiletries. A polite screw brought me that evening's menu: a choice of roast turkey and stuffing, spaghetti bolognaise, or a vegetarian dish. He returned a few minutes later with a complimentary copy of that day's *Telegraph*. Had I booked onto a luxury cruise?

Marine heaven continued for three more days during which I read books from the well-stocked prison library and drew and painted the splendid view across Portland harbour. I had to pinch myself to make sure I wasn't dreaming. This had to be the most cushy establishment in the whole of the prison service. No wonder, as the governor mendaciously claimed in a notorious *Sun* article, no inmate had ever requested a transfer.

It was too good to last, of course. Reality replaced false paradise four days after we boarded. We were abruptly and brutally told to pack up all our things and proceed to the A4 landing, the noisiest and most violent – 'boisterous' was the screws' euphemism – on HMP Weare. I was given an inner (no sea-view) cabin with yet another drug addict – the entire boat was awash with drugs – who played his music at full volume and danced round in the nude. On my first evening, I was 'kidnapped' by five enormous black men at the far end of the landing and made to play chess with them. They told me they would 'beat the living shit out of you, Whitey' if I won – or even if I lost. I kept my nerve and shrewdly went for a stalemate, so they let me go. Another evening, they challenged me to Scrabble, but bottled out when they realised how good I was.

Life aboard the floating prison slowly evolved into a weird rhythm of its own. We could feel the heave and swell during the summer storms, but nobody was ever seasick. HMP Weare would be hell for anyone who suffers from claustrophobia, since apart from one's 'cabin' and a minute association area with a single pool table, there was absolutely nowhere to go. All the air was recycled, which was fine until the air-conditioning broke down, which it frequently did. Ditto the toilets. Exercise was difficult to get because it invariably clashed with other activities. One Saturday morning, I took it all alone in the rain on top deck, the only one of 400 prisoners to do so. (The screws solemnly stood guard over me.) Due to the cramped conditions, everything had to be carefully organised, which was fine until the computer broke down – again, not uncommon – and then the boat became confusion at sea.

Education, presided over by a scatterbrained naval wife, was particularly chaotic. I won't pretend I didn't enjoy the art classes (we had two excellent teachers, Nina and Judith, and three hours in their studio was like being given 'shore leave' for the afternoon) but, due to computer failure, one never knew which class one was supposed to be at, and prisoners wandered around the boat like lost souls in limbo and then found themselves being put on report for being out of bounds.

Worst of all was the sheer boredom and an odd feeling of being manipulated; at times, it felt like actual sensory deprivation. I am not so paranoid as to think that this was a deliberate ploy on the part of the prison authorities, but it was hard not to believe that one was a guinea pig in some kind of penal experiment. (HMP Weare has been adjudged a 'success', whatever that means, and two more floating prisons are to join it soon.)

I was unlucky with my ship- (cell-)mates. After the crack addict and the nude dancer, there was a Scots burglar named Phil who claimed to have an original Turner hidden away in his loft insulation. Worst of all was a particularly vicious young car thief named Montgomery, known as Full Monty for his habit of playing 'rave' music at full volume all day and all night. I couldn't handle this (or him) for very long, so arranged to move to another cell with a very sulky inmate named Ian. When I asked him what he was in for, he replied 'Murder' – the only word he addressed to me in four weeks.

From other sources I learned that Ian had tried to blow his wife's lover's head off with a shotgun, a crime of passion which, in 'Lucky' Court 13 at the Old Bailey, had earned him only three years. I tried not to think about this more than once a day.

Most of the inmates on HMP Weare were hardened criminals reaching the end of long sentences, and so not wanting too much trouble. The officers had all volunteered to work on the ship and, with the usual exceptions, had a pleasant and helpful attitude. My personal officer, Mr Phillpott, was well-meaning, if ineffectual, and there was another, Steve Hallett, whom I would happily employ as a valet if ever I make it rich. I was genuinely sorry to say goodbye to him when I left. I had an ambivalent relationship with one officer, known all over the ship as Little Hitler. Small of stature, and not unlike Adolf in appearance, he was one of those curious individuals who manages to be both absurd and sinister at the same time. He remained deeply suspicious of me for many weeks until one day, checking the mail, he discovered that we shared the same rather upmarket local solicitor. From then on, he couldn't do enough for me. (He was to be further impressed by personal notes from the newly ennobled Melvyn Bragg, an old friend, and from *The Oldie* editor – thank you, by the way, to those readers who wrote to me on board.)

The jewel in the crown on the ship was the thrice-weekly chaplaincy service. With a Roman Catholic Mass on Friday, Anglican church on Sunday, a chaplain's class on Tuesday, one was never more than two days away from spiritual consolation. I liked all the chaplains, but Bill Cave, the Anglican (all Anglican prison chaplains are called Bill) was in a class of his own. He had once been a university chaplain but didn't consider ministering to 400 tattooed gorillas with drug problems to be a step down.

Towards the end of my sentence, I was sent on a P-R (Pre-Release) course, two-thirds of which was spent watching videos about conditions in other prisons. When I complained to the officer

23

in charge about the relevance of this, he said: 'Well, 75 per cent of the guys will be coming back soon, so they might as well know what to expect.' How cynical can you get?

One Tuesday evening in July, Bill Cave asked me to give a talk on God, which I did, reaching the rather unexpected conclusion that I had felt closer to Him during these two months in the steel womb of HMP Weare than in any other period of my interesting life. After all, in the womb one either sinks or swims, dies or grows, and I think I most definitely swam and grew during this summer. As Peter Ustinov said of his time in the Army, I loathed every moment of it, and I wouldn't have missed it for the world.

Going Straight at Last?

Twenty years ago, the Rev Bill Cave-Browne-Cave, chaplain aboard HMP Weare (the 'floating prison' in which I was incarcerated for two months this summer) was chairman of a quasi-religious charitable organisation dedicated to helping the homeless. Knowing me to be in that category, he suggested that, on my release, I should seek their help. He even wrote a letter on my behalf to their director, a Mr Etherington-Smith. I, too, wrote to Mr Etherington-Smith, but neither of us received a reply.

On the day of my release, 14 August, several phone calls, including one from a mobile on the train between Dorset and London, elicited the information that the hostel was, indeed, expecting me. This was just as well, since a sexy blonde I met on the train proposed that we alight at Bournemouth and spend 'quality time' together in a posh hotel. I was extremely tempted but resisted her offer and resolved to play it straight, for once in my life.

Arriving in Cambridge at 2.30 on a very hot afternoon, I ignored the chaplain's advice to save my pennies and took a taxi from the station to the charity's head office (it's true that I had only the £47 discharge grant, but I was carrying all the paintings I had done in prison). Mr Etherington-Smith had gone on holiday, but his minions again assured me that I was expected.

The taxi took me on to an unprepossessing hostel in North Cambridge, later to be christened 'the hostel from hell', where there were no staff on duty and nobody to receive me. I killed several hours in the company of the kind of people I should prefer not to describe until a 'voluntary worker', a youth of unbelievable callowness named Johnnie, showed me to a filthy little room with no bedding, no towel, no coat hangers, no waste-paper basket. There was no paper in the dirty toilet and no prospect of any, he said.

This disgusting place became my 'home' for the next two weeks. At night I was kept awake by dozens of drunken, narcotic-crazed youths running up and down the stairs, shouting and slamming the fire doors, of which there were many. They played the TV at full volume all through the night. (Most of them didn't even live in the house, but were 'guests' of people who did.) It had been a good deal quieter in prison, for which I soon began to feel quite nostalgic. I seemed, as usual, to have gone from the frying-pan into the fire and I couldn't help remembering the beautiful, clean, free French *foyers* just across the Channel. (This hostel wanted £108 a week rent to live in these conditions.)

On the Monday morning, I duly presented myself at the nearby Job Centre (DHSS) and was given a mountain of forms to fill in and an interview time for the following Saturday. At this, on learning that I had lived abroad and just come out of prison, they gave me another ten forms to complete – but no money. (Finally, after another delay, they sent me a Giro for £50, which got stolen by the residents of the hostel, along with all the rest of my post.)

Cambridge, of course, was swarming with foreign tourists and – so far as I was concerned – with ghosts from the past. Forty years ago, I used to come across from 'the other place' to attend parties given by the late and great Peter Cook and his girlfriend, later wife, Wendy Snowden. And did I not once see Jonathan Miller, strutting, peacock-like in his vanity, along King's Parade? This time, I ran into another ghost, a live one: Dr George 'Dadie' Rylands being pushed in his wheelchair by his carer across Kings Court on his way to lunch. Ninety-six and still going strong, and an *Oldie* reader to boot! Truly, this was turning out to be a dance to the music of time.

It was the flesh that saved me when the spirit grew weak. Desperate for female company after months of incarceration, I began a flirtation with an attractive 26-year-old visitor to the hostel, Joyce, who turned out to have a friend, Anna, who worked for 'Cold Winter Rescue', an emergency housing organisation/association. Within 48 hours, I had moved into a tiny, brutally modern house in the existential wilderness of the Arbury estate in North Cambridge. My new housemates were Marcus, a pathetic little alcoholic, and Sean, a gentle, tattooed giant whose girlfriend, Juliet, was an art teacher – which was what I was looking for. Just for one brief moment, I thought my life might be taking a turn for the better...

But the Arbury estate, two miles from the town centre, very soon got me down. Buses, supposed to run every ten minutes, were less than half-hourly. Waiting for one in the early morning rain (autumn had come early to East Anglia), I watched a fat blonde mother with a ring through her nose cuffing and shouting at her squalling brats, and I began to wonder what on earth I was doing here. Why stay in a country which has gone as ragged at the edges as this one when I could be enjoying life back in la belle France? (which is probably where I shall be by the time you read this).

Then there is the question of money. Have you tried living on £47 a week? l require a minimum of £100, which means that I am currently shoplifting food at the rate of £53 per week. Sooner or later, of course, I will get caught, and my solicitor tells me that I am 'looking at' 12 months in HMP next time. But would that be so bad? Twelve months, in real terms, means six months, which would just take care of the winter – a dry roof over my head and plentiful, if unadventurous, food in my stomach. Sex? Well, I can do without it, as I have done for some years now.

I write this in the knowledge that, once again, I have jumped through all the hoops that society is holding up for me. I have tried to 'go straight' and I have failed. The system, whatever that is, has failed me, too. How people with less resources than myself manage in these circumstances I just cannot imagine. Yet I am not down-hearted; in fact, I remain strangely cheerful and optimistic. There is a world elsewhere. At least, I think there is. Anyway, I will keep you informed.

Brighton:
The Last Resort?

My request for *Oldie* readers to write to me on the prison boat (*Oldie* 114) brought in a deluge of replies with many interesting and gratifying consequences. One lady with a long address in Wales – though not, I suspect, Welsh herself, since she seemed to share my contempt for that race – wrote me a long series of dazzlingly perceptive letters, then suddenly complained that my replies were too brief and insufficiently self-revealing. I was driven to plead fatigue after addressing the envelopes.

Another, Margaret from Shaftesbury in Dorset, sent £10 and asked me to pray, at Mass, for her daughter, travelling in Germany, and for herself, travelling to South America. I did so, and, to the best of my knowledge, no harm befell either of them. Margaret and I have arranged to meet for lunch, though I don't know whether that will now happen.

There must be a large concentration of readers in the Brighton area because several letters reached me from there, including one from William Garnett – I don't think he will mind my giving his name [Maybe not, but I have changed it anyway – Ed] – offering to buy me a drink at the Royal Albion Hotel should I ever find myself in Brighton, which I did early in September. Arriving at the Royal Albion, I found a small, dark-suited man nervously washing the perspiration off his hands in the downstairs Gents. When I asked him what was up, he replied, 'Well, I'm about to meet Wilfred De'Ath!' I explained that I was he and he looked visibly relieved. Obviously, I don't look like the monster of legend.

I took a couple of Bloody Marys off Mr Garnett, and I would have had a third if he hadn't had to be back in his office. He confirmed my impression that there are many avid *Oldie* fans in the Brighton and Hove district. They even meet up from time to time at the Royal Thistle Hotel. Mr Garnett expressed his disappointment that at one such gathering a few years ago, attended by the editor, by the late Willie Rushton, and by Enfield Senior, he had failed to meet Auberon Waugh who, due to unforeseen circumstances, had not turned up. I told Mr Garnett that this was a disappointment that I could have lived with.

The most pleasing letter of all also came from the South Coast, from Jimmy Osborne of Seaford, a retired racecourse bookmaker, who offered to meet me by car at the prison ship on the morning of my release. I declined this kind offer because I have a horror of driving with total strangers. But Mr Osborne persisted and eventually drove all the way to Cambridge to pick me up to spend a few days in his delightful flat.

On the face of it, Jimmy Osborne and I have little in common. I have never been near a racecourse in my life, and wouldn't for the life of me know how to lay a bet, or whatever the expression is. Gambling has never been one of my many vices. But Jimmy turned out to be an extremely literate bookmaker with all the books – real ones – that I have ever wanted to read lining the walls of his well-appointed flat. He gave me the run of the place for a few days and I felt extremely happy there. Now he says that I can go down to Seaford whenever I want while I search for permanent accommodation in Brighton, and that thought – the thought of having the run of his flat yet again – makes me extremely happy, of course.

On our first evening in Seaford, Jimmy took me along to Wetherspoons along the coast in Hove, a pub which was full of old men, who had clearly seen better days, sitting at separate tables gazing into their beers while they waited for someone to buy them another one. Many of these oldies were retired actors who managed to make one drink last all evening. The place filled me with horror. The prospect of ending up like that in ten years' time is almost more than I can bear. Perhaps that is why my new friend Jimmy took me there – as a warning to what will become of me if I don't go straight. Or even if I do.

More cheerfully, on the Sunday evening we went along to a pub quiz, at a place called the Connaught, where I met another *Oldie* reader, a delightful Irishman called Stephen. I have always rather conceitedly fancied myself as Brain of Britain where pub quizzes are concerned, but this time I didn't do so well because the standard was unbelievably high, so much so that I fell flat on my face in front of all my new friends. But so what? It's nice to know that I can go down to Brighton whenever I want and be among such friends. I am starting to hate Cambridge, where I am living, so I guess Brighton might turn out to be the last resort for me. Otherwise, I'll go back to France.

Towards the end of September, I stole a copy of *The Oldie* from the Cambridge branch of WH Smith's to send to an oldie lag on the prison ship. I was immediately collared, tapped on the shoulder by an elderly Scotsman whom I took to be the store detective.

I thought I was being arrested for shoplifting and visions of six or 12 months at Her Majesty's Pleasure for stealing *The Oldie* swam through my guilty, fevered imagination. But all he said was, 'That's the best publication around. Good luck to you.'

Phew! Call me Old Brown Nose, but I agree with the oldie Scot –
it is the best publication around and the readers who wrote to me
aboard the floating prison have, with the usual exceptions,
turned out to be absolute bricks.

A Day in the Life of the Scrounger

Michel, the *foyer*'s director, wakes me at 6.30am. An ex-boxer, allegedly homosexual, he spends just a little too long staring as I get washed and dressed. But what can I do? For some years, he has protected me from the anti-British sentiments of the other residents of the Abri de Limoges. In many ways, he is like a brother to me.

I do not linger over breakfast. Aida, the *foyer* tart, is staring balefully at me over the bitter coffee and croissants. Having recently lost her rich protector, she presumably now wants back the several hundred francs she 'lent' me in the spring when I was broke – as I still am. I know for a fact that she carries a knife in her handbag and that she knows some very rough chaps in town.

I walk through the silent, still-dark streets to 8 o'clock Mass at St Michel-des-Lions. The priest is fat and pompous and wears a monocle. He viciously kicks the hapless altar boy when he stands in the wrong place. But his sacristan, an old lady, greets me warmly. Sometimes I am even asked to read the lesson in my impeccable French. After Mass I slip across to the Hotel Royal Limousin – supposedly the best hotel in town but, in fact, a dump – to make use of their toilet facilities; 49 times out of 50, they don't mind. The 50th time, they throw me out.

At nine, I proceed to the Secours Catholique (a Catholic charity) for a second, more substantial breakfast of baguette and butter, two types of sausage, pâté, ham, quiche lorraine, cheeses, jam, croissants, brioches, gateaux and, of course, lashings of hot, black coffee. The food is excellent, but the company – mostly smelly tramps and drunks – execrable. The Secours Catholique also has a well-stocked *vestiaire* which will clothe you for nothing. This time they've given me a superb winter coat which makes me look like a French Cabinet Minister.

I steal a copy of the *Guardian*'s international edition – a less heinous crime than it sounds in a city where the rebellious *lycéens* are constantly looting the shops. At ten, it's time to meet up with my two friends, Raymond and Jacques. Raymond is an expatriate American, aged 74, stranded here in deep provincial France. Jacques, 68, is Aida's former protector, a retired civil servant, and still a rich man despite having spent close to one million francs (£100,000) on her, mostly for clothes, over 18 months.

We three drink coffee and gossip and attempt the hard crossword in Ray's copy of the *International Herald Tribune*. At 11, I proceed to Jauvion, Limoges's restaurant social, probably the best value in France, if not in Europe, where for seven francs (70 pence) I eat: soup, an entree (usually pâté or a salad), a main course (usually meat with pasta), cheese, fruit, gâteau, coffee. Unbelievably good though, again, the company leaves a great deal to be desired.

At 11.45 or so, I go to meet *le facteur* (the postman) but he very rarely has anything for me from the old country. There are times when the pains of exile are hard to bear. If it isn't actually raining in Limoges (which it usually is) I take my siesta at 12 on a park bench outside the magnificent new library. My headmaster used to say that I would end up on a park bench (if not on the gallows) and so he has been proved right.

Limoges has spent billions of francs on its new library, which must be one of the largest in Europe. It has everything – a cafeteria, a winter garden, a state-of-the-art computer system, an amazing collection of CDs – except new books. A typical piece of Gallic vaingloriousness, the triumph of style over substance. Everybody, staff and customers alike, feels bewildered and over-whelmed by the sheer scale of it.

At 3pm, Ray and I, despairing of the expensive library cafeteria, set out to Flunch, one of a chain of restaurants all over France, for cheap tea with lemon. Flunch is full of old ladies, mostly widows, who stare fixedly at us. Perhaps they are looking for second (or third) husbands. Perhaps there is a chance here for me, after all.

Later, we catch the dying rays of the autumn sun on another park bench in Place Stalingrad. Imagine a place called that in Britain! It is, in some ways, stimulating to live where memories of the Second World War are still fresh.

At 6.30, I return to the *foyer* – after a few beers paid for by Ray – and pay my one franc for one more night. My heart is in my mouth to see if it is Françoise or Annie who will be serving our supper. If it is Françoise, the meal will be over by 7.30 or so. If it is Annie, who is slow and engages every tramp, drunk, and neurotic in prolonged conversation, it could go on until 9 o'clock. (Both of these young ladies are in love with me, of course. And who can blame them?)

We eat: tomato soup, cassoulet, cheese, fruit compote, gateaux. For one franc! My entire day on the scrounge in Limoges has cost me precisely 8 francs (80 pence).

And so to an early bed in my austere bedroom, which sometimes I have to myself or sometimes have to share with a French gentleman of the road. I glance briefly at *Paris Match* or the new *Oldie*, then slip into a fitful sleep with disturbingly 'gay' dreams in which Michel finally has his way with me. Ah well. In the 19th century, any French army officer in disgrace was offered the choice of being cashiered or posted to Limoges. The adjective *limogé* has now entered the language, meaning to be exiled. And that is what I now am: in exile.

Getting Away
With it All

Arecent unpleasant though not entirely unexpected
encounter with the French police (they dragged me off a
TGV at Dax, south of Bordeaux, drove me to the *sûreté*,
and threatened me with two months' imprisonment, pending
appeal, for hotel offences dating back to 1996) has sent my
mind spinning back to the many other times this has happened
to me...

It all began in Normandy during the long, hot summer of
1992, when I mistimed a Sunday afternoon exit from a small
hotel in Caen and was spotted by the proprietor's wife who was
sitting in a nearby café. She sent her husband up to the station
on his motorcycle and he got me arrested for non-payment of
his bill.

The Caen police were pretty agreeable (there was even one
who spoke English) but kept me awake, Gestapo fashion, all
through one night in an ultra-modern cell by shining a bright
light in my face. Next morning, breakfastless, I was transferred
in handcuffs to a kind of cage underneath the office of the
Procureur de la Republique (State Prosecutor) who, after
commenting sarcastically, 'I suppose even in England – *même en
Angleterre* – people usually settle their hotels bills,' ordered the
gendarmes to release me. Legal proceedings followed, but I
never bothered to turn up.

Three weeks later, in Angers, I was in trouble again over a

5,000 franc (£500) hotel bill, but the extremely young, bull-like police inspector let me go after an hour or so's interview – he clearly understood that I had not a sou in the whole wide world and that there was very little prospect of the bill being paid. There was no legal follow-up in this case.

I managed to keep out of trouble (in France, at any rate) until Christmas 1993 when, staying with some nuns in Lourdes, I was falsely accused of desecrating their chapel and making off with 2,000 francs. The inspector, again very young, was extremely nervous, not to say neurotic, a dead ringer for Inspector Clouseau. (He kept, apologetically, borrowing my pen and then forgetting to give it back. He was also very shocked to find a copy of *Playboy* in my room, as though that, in itself, were incriminating evidence.)

When asked if I had ever received psychiatric treatment, I said, 'No, but I wouldn't mind some.' To my surprise, he indicated that they gave it right there in the gendarmerie. 'What, here in the police station?' I naively enquired. 'Yes, follow me.' He took me down a corridor and pointed at a completely bare, windowless cell. 'This is where we give it,' he said. 'We make the suspect strip naked and then we beat the living shit out of him.' In the end, after six hours of interrogation, this sadistic Clouseau was obliged to let me go for lack of evidence.

In July 1994, I myself called in the police in Forcalquier, Alpes de Haute Provence, when a suspicious hotel-keeper, who didn't like the look of my cheque, threatened to throw me out of a first-floor window. I was held in custody overnight and woke up the next morning, which happened to be my 57th birthday, in a kind of dungeon under the local castle. An extremely young trainee policeman (he was doing his National Service, which you can do in the police force in France), to whom I complained that, 'This is supposed to be the land of liberty,' agreed and at once set me free. He did more than that. He drove me to the *Mairie* (town hall) where they gave me 150 francs (about £15) and a bus voucher to Avignon, my next destination. He even bought me lunch! Now that is the kind of police force we should have over here.

In Macon (September 1995) the police were, again, on my side. I ordered, and ate, an extremely expensive meal, with suitable wines, in a very posh hotel, then discovered that I had no money to pay for it. The malignant chef/proprietor at once called in two gendarmes who, to my intense satisfaction, insisted that he tear up the bill in front of me. I wonder if I could work that one again...

Arrested again in Sablé-sur-Sarthe in April 1997, I finally decided to make a clean breast of all the hotels I had 'done' in France over five years. I can't remember how many it came to, but I know that the sum involved totalled 68,000 francs (£7,000). For this, I received a three-month suspended sentence from a court in Le Mans. (In England, I would have been 'looking at' at least two years, not suspended, for offences in that sum.) So I suppose there is something to be said for French justice after all.

Now, in Dax, I'm in trouble yet again. They're not going to suspend it this time. The young inspector (why are they all so young? Or is it that I'm getting old?) gave a fine display of anti-British sentiment in the course of our interview. His general line throughout was: 'Do you really regard us French policemen as complete imbeciles?' (Note the French sense of inferiority *vis-à-vis* the British police.) Of course, I was tempted to say 'Yes', but that might have angered him even more. He did, however, crack one joke; at least I think it was meant to be a joke. Leaving me in his office for a moment, he said, 'Please don't steal anything from my desk.' Well, French humour was never up to much.

Finally, as always in my French experience, he had to let me go. 'Am I free?' I asked. 'Free as air,' he replied, 'until next March.'

Contempt of Court

The first time I appeared in a magistrates' court was in October 1990 at Chipping Norton, Oxfordshire. The court had no custody suite, so I was held for some hours in a kind of broom cupboard while the other cases were heard. The magistrate, a local dentist's wife, was totally inarticulate and had to be told what to say by the clerk of the court. (She sent me to the old Oxford prison, now closed, for seven days.)

Things got a little better in Banbury, a more sophisticated set-up, the following week, but not much. This time, the presiding beak was a local estate agent (they often become magistrates for some reason), who granted the police 72 hours to question me about a single hotel offence. (This is the time they are allowed to question a mass-murderer or a suspected terrorist.) I began to think, as I have often thought since, that in a magistrates' court the dice might be a shade loaded in favour of the prosecution...

In Oxford, in an even more sophisticated court, where I appeared in 1991, the Chairman, an Oxford don, turned out to be an old drinking companion of mine, so naturally he had to stand down. The two terrified 'book-ends', the lady magistrates on either side of him, were so nervous at the prospect of deciding my fate that they sent the matter (impersonating a police officer, which I had done in an Oxford pub as a joke) up to the Crown Court for sentencing. That meant I had to hang around the university city for four months before being given a suspended sentence by Judge Crawford, Head of the Oxford and Midland Circuit, and another pair of alarmed lady 'book-ends' who were sitting with him.

41

Broadly speaking, in the criminal justice system, the further you are from London, the worse treatment you get. In Portsmouth, in 1992, I was kept in one of a series of iron cages beneath the magistrates' court which had been constructed to hold drunken sailors and other criminals during the Napoleonic Wars. I got a message to a friend of mine, David Stancliffe, the Provost of Portsmouth Cathedral, now Bishop of Salisbury, and asked him to send me a pair of shoes, since the police had managed to lose mine. His charming wife Sarah brought them along and was horrified by the conditions in which I was being held, together with several other unfortunates. She promised to ask David to protest about them, but – to the best of my knowledge – he never did.

In Exeter, in 1993, I appeared in front of the wife of the local Tory MP; she was wearing the traditional woman magistrate's large, flowery hat. (The men always sport half-moon spectacles, I've noticed.) She told me in a plummy voice that she was sending me to prison for four months on the grounds that I had committed a 'deliberate' offence. As if such an offence (an unpaid hotel bill) could be anything other than deliberate.

In Salisbury, in 1995, I stood in the dock in the very court used by Judge Jeffreys to send people to the gallows. It was not a good omen. The vindictive woman magistrate, a local busybody who had somehow or other got herself made JP, told me that she didn't believe in 'community' sentencing (probation or community service) for hardened criminals like myself, but only in imprisonment. So I got sent down again...

All courts are meant to be 'people's courts', but in reality they are run on strictly philistine lines by the Lord Chancellor's department. The ushers are generally sour and disagreeable, and the clerks of the court unspeakably obtuse and stupid. Only rarely are there any facilities in magistrates' courts – toilets, refreshment areas, nappy-changing arrangements – which might make them user-friendly. You hang around for hours in an infinitely depressing environment, along with some of the dregs of society, and are then sent to prison or made to pay a hefty fine to keep the Lord Chancellor's department afloat. (The solicitors and barristers give themselves excellent facilities, of course.)

I am sorry to sound bitter, and I have to admit that, just occasionally, it does go my way. In Eastbourne, in 1996, I was given a conditional discharge for shoplifting by a very nice lady magistrate. Appearing in the same court a year later for breaching a Probation Order, I was offered the choice of a £25 fine or staying in the precincts of the court until the end of business. Since it was a Saturday morning, when business finishes at 1pm, and since my case was heard at 12.45, it was not a hard decision, and I felt I'd got off lightly for once.

The only other civilised court I know, outside London and Oxford, is, unexpectedly, Dorchester, where I appeared last year in a very pleasant, modern committee room. The magistrate, however, was of the old school, as one might have known. A pompous little man (an estate agent, again) he declined to accept my excuse for FTA (Failure to Appear at an earlier hearing) that I had not be able to afford the £58 day-return rail fare. Was I expected to walk, or hitch-hike? He was also livid that I refused to co-operate with a psychiatric report on the grounds that I found the person writing it to be a congenital idiot. So he gave me six months.

Now I'm back in court again – for the 35th time in ten years – in Brighton, a reasonably enlightened place (they have a non-alcoholic drinks trolley) where I'm looking at an 'exemplary' sentence of 12 months for shoplifting – the most severe sentence a magistrates' court can give. It may not come to that, of course, but if it does, I shall keep my head down and do my time, and then I shall write to Mr Blair and ask him: whatever became of the notion of the people's court?

One Lump or Two?

At long, long last l have a decent probation officer, Peter Tye. When I arrive at his Brighton office, Mr Tye is always on time; always greets me warmly; always makes me coffee with his own fair hands and asks 'One lump or two, Mr De'Ath?'. All this is in such marked contrast to my previous experience of the East Sussex Probation service that I have to pinch myself to make sure I'm not dreaming…

In Eastbourne, in 1996, I had a man named Charles, working-class but a pleasant enough cove, who turned up punctually roughly 50 per cent of the time. For 25 per cent of our appointments he didn't turn up at all. I was sometimes referred to a callow girl named Lorraine who insisted on trying to make me feel 'remorse' for my so-called crimes ie. not paying hotel bills. 'What am I supposed to do,' I asked her once in exasperation, 'prostrate myself on your office carpet and weep with remorse for my victims, the shareholders of large hotel groups or of the insurance companies who cover them for theft?'

Because I refused to indulge in such hypocrisies, Lorraine was extremely severe with me when it came to writing my pre-sentence report. She said that I felt no remorse for my offences – perfectly true – which didn't, of course, go down at all well with the magistrates. Because I refused to lie and say I did feel remorse when I didn't, they gave me an extra three months' imprisonment. Once you have allowed yourself to be swallowed up in the great wave of the criminal justice system, you cannot win.

Given all this, it is hard to know what I shall find to talk about with Mr Tye. He is the first probation officer I have had who is prepared to accept that mine is essentially a victimless crime. Not paying hotel bills is, so far as I am concerned, a simple matter of economics. Hotel debts are no different from any other kind of debt. Mr Tye is also the first probation officer to accept that I am not suffering from any mental or personality disorder and am therefore not in need of the East Sussex forensic psychiatric service, which consists of one rather dim-witted community psychiatric nurse brandishing a hypodermic needle.

So what are Mr Tye and I going to talk about? My reminiscences of other probation officers and services perhaps? The Oxfordshire officer who insisted on calling me 'sir' because he said I made him feel inferior in every conceivable way, socially, intellectually, even sartorially, whenever I entered his office; the Berkshire bail hostel supervisor who sported a brush haircut and an earring and drove a souped-up motorbike whom I persistently mistook for one of his own residents; the sexy divorcee trainee (Oxford again) who 'came on' to me in the bail hostel one dark winter night, then turned the tables and accused me of 'sexual harrassment' when I complained to her boss. As you will have gathered, I do not have a high opinion of the probation service or of the calibre of officer they are recruiting these days – a little above the average policeman or prison officer, perhaps, but not much.

So here we go again. Brighton, to my relief, seems a bit of an improvement on all these other places. Mike Teague, a delightful Scot with a good sense of humour, wrote an extremely perceptive pre-sentence report which saved me from jail, though he, too, is chronically unpunctual and sometimes fails to turn up.

Meanwhile, Peter Tye and I have solved the problem of how to pass the time. I am dictating my memoirs to him. I have just told him what it was like being brought up by a German mother in war-torn London, a recipe for subsequent schizoid tendencies if ever there was one. I had Peter eating out of my hand. Next time, we shall get on to the trauma of doing National Service in

Germany ten years after the war when I was still, notionally, the enemy. That, with my luck, should have him kneeling on his threadbare carpet weeping the tears of remorse they have been trying to extract from me. A slight reversal of roles, of course, but much more productive. Memoirs written while you wait!

Home Thoughts
From a Fraud

I knew that Brighton was full of gangsters – I've read *Brighton Rock* – but I didn't expect to find one on my doorstep. On 12 March last, I was sitting down to a quiet supper when a bearded heavy, built like a brick shithouse, who seemed to have stepped out of a British B-picture of the postwar era, hands deep in the pockets of his 1950s-style gabardine raincoat, entered my flat and ordered me out of town. He didn't give a reason and I didn't stop to look for one. I packed up very quickly indeed and took a taxi to a rather horrible hotel – unusually for me, I had money on me – where I spent one night before taking a train along the coast to St Leonards-on-Sea which, unexpectedly, was also full of criminals…

Prominent among these was one Guiy de Montfort, with whom I was 'banged up' on the prison ship HMP Weare last year. Normally, I hate other criminals, but de Montfort is an exception. His real name is Graham Leaver (he's the son of an NCO from Deptford), but he calls himself de Montfort to aid his speciality, which is setting up fraudulent multimedia companies and then persuading rich, vulnerable women to invest in them. He has enjoyed considerable success with this, in America and over here, but at present he's having rather a thin time, courtesy of Nigel Dempster, who constantly writes about his actives in the *Daily Mail*. So the British authorities have got wise to him.

I spent three days in Guiy's penthouse flat – like many criminals he can be surprisingly hospitable – before moving in, at his suggestion, with one of his victims, an ex-heroin addict named Barbara who had foolishly invested £4,000 in the con man. So I spent a few more days in her rather pleasant sea-facing flat until she got understandably fed up with feeding and watering me for nothing; the realisation slowly dawning on her that all that was happening was that Guiy's debt to her was increasing.

It was time to move on, so I jumped the Hastings train to Victoria, then another one to Oxford, where I arrived without a penny but not without a prayer, which I said to Our Blessed Lady and, lo and behold, there was a purse containing £40 on the seat right in front of me. Just enough for a luxury bed-and-breakfast which kept me going until I could meet up with my friend, the ex-Bodleian librarian Derek Day, who advanced me £100 with which to return to France. (It was Derek's 60th birthday and, as I pointed out to him, there is no better way of celebrating than giving money to an old friend.)

I caught a rapid train down to Portsmouth, then a taxi, and just made the 14:30 sailing to Caen. Oh, the blessed relief of being back in la belle France. A superb night's sleep in a small hotel, another rapide down to Le Mans, then the TGV to Angers and a stopping train to Saumur where the Foyer des Quatre Saisons welcomes me with open arms. I swore I'd never return there, but I've been proved wrong, and the first night's menu explains why: celery salad, fricassee of turkey with spaghetti, pistachio cream ... another meal to die for.

I've burned my boats in England now, having breached a probation order, but I just don't care any more. There are, in any case, only three things about England I miss: television, pubs and the British sense of humour. French television is terrible. I've looked at more interesting wallpaper. (Mind you, Swiss television is even worse. I once insulted some friends in Lausanne by asking why they were showing children's programmes at 10pm.) French bars are all very well, but they are all the same and become monotonous after a while. I miss those long nocturnal drives into the Oxfordshire countryside in search of an authentic country pub with a real log fire and real ale...

The French do have a sense of humour of a kind, but I've never been able to penetrate it. They certainly have no sense of irony. Years ago, during the Mitterrand Presidency, when it was widely rumoured that le beau François spent his time cavorting with prostitutes in the Elysée Palace, a friend and I were walking through a remote Brittany town and came upon a very old-fashioned, Bill Tidy-type prostitute (patched tights, ill-applied lipstick, fag in mouth) leaning against a wall. 'Who's she waiting for? Francois Mitterrand?' I would have asked had my friend been English, but since he was French, I kept my mouth shut. One never knows. A true republican, he might have accused me of insulting his President. It is sometimes a little frustrating not being able to say whichever ironical quip comes to mind.

However, all this is a very small price to pay for living in such a beautiful and enlightened country as France. This time I have no plans to return.

Healing Words

I spent the winter of 1992–93 with some sisters of the Immaculate Conception in their convent just outside Lourdes. From my balcony I could see the foothills of the Pyrenees and hear the swift rushing water of the River Gave. It was, in many respects, the happiest and most peaceful time of my life. The sisters fed and watered me but, most of the time, they left me alone with my thoughts. We said Mass every morning and in the afternoon I walked through the forest to the Grotto to pay my respects to Our Lady, to whom I developed a devotion which has never since left me.

The time came to move on to the great city of Toulouse, and the sensation of peace evaporated; though I have been back to Lourdes many times since, it has never fully returned. I am grateful to Ruth Harris's excellent book (*Lourdes-Allen Lane*) for giving me an opportunity to express my real feelings about the place.

In her first chapter, Ms Harris mentions 'the mingling of spirituality and commercialism' that has always characterised Lourdes, and it would be easy for a cynical journalist like myself to dismiss it as one set of credulous peasants – pilgrims – being systematically ripped off by another set of grasping ones – shopkeepers. But there is more to it than that. In fact, the 'commercial' aspect of Lourdes is one of the many myths about the place. The authorities have been at pains to keep sanctuary and shops well apart and, speaking for myself, I have never purchased anything in Lourdes nor ever felt pressed to do so.

So were the apparitions 'true' or were they merely the externalised projections of the sickly adolescent, Bernadette

Soubirous? Whether or not they possessed any objective reality (I suspect not), they have given rise to an extremely powerful myth, one that has already endured for 150 years and seems likely to continue. (One might equally argue that Christianity itself is a 'myth' that continues to make itself felt as though in response to some deep need in the human psyche.)

The Virgin has, allegedly, already appeared more than 50 times in France (but never in England – the French jeer that she doesn't care for our weather!), invariably singling out the ignorant, the poverty-stricken, the rural and the dispossessed. Putting myself firmly in the second category, that of the poor, I would have to own up to an ever-increasing devotion to her, so the events of 1858 in Lourdes come as no surprise to me. If you had told me 20 years ago, in 1979, the year in which I converted to Roman Catholicism, that by far my most precious possession today would be a simple silver medallion of Our Lady, I would have called you mad, but that is certainly the case. At another level, this may be interpreted as a devotion to the 'female' principle in life, which has also been of great assistance in my search for a spiritual dimension…

Our Lady, I believe, has seen me through many vicissitudes and difficult passages. The medallion, which was given to me by a very holy man in Lourdes about five years ago, undoubtedly possesses healing powers, which brings us on to the question of the miraculous healings of Lourdes. Here l am happy to settle for the platitude which says that, whereas very few are actually healed, many are helped and that the whole ambience of the place is so wonderful that the suffering and the dying cannot but be cheered and encouraged by it.

Ruth Harris herself went on a pilgrimage to Lourdes. What she saw and experienced there touched but did not convert her: indeed, she says that the open-mindedness and spiritual generosity of the people she met only served to confirm her in her Jewish secularism. Nevertheless, the visit to Lourdes completely changed her approach to the subject and by writing a book that is neither a Catholic apology nor an anti-clerical tirade she has done us all a service by offering a study that differs radically from many previous accounts. This involves no naive claim to 'objectivity', but provides a valuable context for believers and, for non-believers, a sense of where the appeal of Lourdes truly lies. Anyway, her book certainly works for me. It is the best general account of the place I have yet read. It even made me feel I should give the sisters of the Immaculate Conception the 8,000 francs I still owe them.

THE VIRGIN IN ENGLAND

Confessions of an Oldie Roué

A friend once perceptively remarked that, as I got older, my women got younger. There was a frightening amount of truth in this observation, so in 1992 I was determined to knock sex on the head by imposing seven years of celibacy on myself. That period expired on 25 March last, since when no girl in France, nay Europe, has been safe

I jest, of course, but not entirely. That witty courtier of Louis XIV who, told of a saint who walked a mile with her guillotined head under her arm, remarked, '*C'est le premier pas qui coûte*' – it's the first step that counts – might have said the same of a time of self-imposed celibacy except that, in this case, it's the first *year* that counts.

In 1993, in Toulouse, I was invited to stay with Claude, a director of Air Inter, the French internal airline, and his ravishing young mistress, Stephanie. One night, Claude had to be out at Blagnac, the Toulouse airport, on business and Stephanie, who had been watching a sexy film on TV and smoking cannabis, tried to tempt me into their bedroom. When I turned her down (she was three months pregnant), she was not at all offended, merely said rather crisply, 'Well, you'll have to do better on Saturday, Wilfred. It's Claude's 30th birthday party and we're inviting a girl from Paris – another Stephanie – especially for you.'

Stephanie Mark II, a student at the Sorbonne, turned out to be even more ravishing than Stephanie Mark I, but she was young enough to be my granddaughter. We dined and danced – but that was all. Once again, I remembered my vow and turned her down. Next morning, I lay in bed and listened to the two Stephanies discussing me over the washing-up. Steph II: '*Et Wilfred, il est pédé ou quoi?*' – Is he queer? Steph I: '*Non, je pense pas*' – No, I don't think so.

On 24 August 1997, while Pope John Paul II was addressing millions of *jeunes* in Paris, I sat in a luxurious Pyrenean villa tentatively stroking the arm of a beautiful young Frenchwoman, Corinne, whose husband happened, just happened, to be away for the day. There had been a long, bibulous lunch; it was very hot. The atmosphere was decidedly erotic. 'It's no good stroking my arm,' said Corinne, crisply again and with Gallic realism. 'You'll have to stroke somewhere else if you're going to get anywhere.'

Just then her mobile phone rang (the husband?); the moment was over and my celibacy saved. There is a God in Heaven, after all.

It's just as well that I've spent these seven years mainly in France, where sex is more openly available than in any other country that I know. I was once asked why there is four times more AIDS in France than in Britain and I replied, almost unthinkingly, that I suppose it was because there is four times as much sexual activity. I have no basis for this statistic and certainly couldn't prove it, but I wouldn't mind betting on it. In France, if you ask a girl out for a drink (*prendre un verre*), she automatically assumes that you intend to sleep with her, and it takes a good deal of courage to extricate oneself, believe me.

I am now used to the fact that daily life in France is full of surprises, many of them pleasant ones, but even I was taken aback when Jean-Marc, the director of the Tarbes *foyer* I'm currently staying in, invited me out to dinner at a restaurant up in the Pyrenees to meet his two pretty daughters. On our way there in the car, he remarked casually: 'Patricia is 26 and Aurelie 14. You may take your choice…' Well, 14 is going it a bit, even by my standards ('Bonjour, M. le Juge!'), but if Patricia, 26, turned out to be beautiful, I knew that I was in deep, deep trouble…

Well, I am in deep, deep trouble. Patricia did, indeed, turn out to be beautiful, with just the sort of dark French looks I adore. She even had an ironical sense of humour, very unusual in a French girl. We hit it off like nobody's business. So at the age of 62 this month (I can pass for younger if the light is right or if there is no light at all) I am back with the oldest game in the world: *chasser la femme*. There is no fool like an oldie fool, of course, and it will almost certainly end in tears, but I'm definitely, as the young say, up for it. Even my almost certain eventual rejection (Patricia is between lovers at present, so I guess I stand a chance) will make a welcome change from boring old celibacy.

At dinner with the girls, Jean-Marc and I had a good deal too much to drink – two litres of peach wine and one of red between us – so he wisely decided not to drive back. We spent the night in a room over the restaurant with the two beauties sleeping in a double bed right next door. Was it really necessary for Patricia to trip *à poil* (naked) through our room on her way to the bathroom? That, of course, is a question to which there is no answer. It is almost more than an oldie *roué* can bear.

Penniless in Provence

Listen hard and you will hear the unmistakable sound of sour grapes being trod. Ten years ago a publisher named Christopher Sinclair-Stevenson sent me a proof copy of *A Year in Provence* since he knew I had once lived there, and asked how many he should print. I replied: 'Three thousand – and you'll still have some left at Christmas.'

How wrong can you be? *A Year in Provence*, boosted by serialisation in the *Sunday Times Magazine*, went on to sell four million copies and made its author, Peter Mayle, a millionaire. He wrote a second (actually better) account of the region, *Toujours Provence*, and that did well too. Last month, I slipped into the English bookshop in Toulouse and stole a copy of his third, *Encore Provence* (Hamish Hamilton, £9.99 paperback – I am ignoring his unreadable novels), to help myself answer a question that has been torturing me since 1989. Why are these little books so successful?

Returning to a place where you have been happy, as Peter Mayle admits and I can confirm, is generally a mistake, yet he and his wife, who went off to America – Long Island – for four years, would seem to have done just that with no noticeable ill effects. True, Mayle quotes the gloomy prescription of Hippocrates: 'Death sits in the bowels; a bad digestion is the root of all evil,' but a bad digestion appears to be the least of Mr Mayle's problems, though one can't help feeling sorry for his stomach, as he begins each gluttonous day with a small glass of olive oil; sets himself up for lunch with alternate layers of butter

57

and thinly sliced French truffles spread on toast, sprinkled with grains of coarse sea salt, accompanied by a glass or two of red wine; actually lunches on charcuterie, cuttlefish poached in saffron broth, cheese and dessert; waits impatiently for dinner time when he puts away several individual crêpes, tarts, plus four pots of pâté, plus a whole mountain of *aligot* (potatoes, cheese, sour cream, garlic), before even approaching his starter (wild mushrooms served in pastry) or his main course, a confit of duck with a circular, golden-brown cake of potatoes, roasted in duck fat and served with garlic and chopped truffles. Cheese (an entire Banon wrapped in chestnut leaves) and dessert (apple crumble and cream) pretty well round things off...

If this is at all typical of a day in the life of Peter Mayle's stomach (and he cheerfully admits that it is – and I've omitted the accompanying wines) then it is nothing short of a miracle that he can still summon the energy to crawl towards, let alone switch on, his word-processor.

By now you will have caught the whiff of those sour grapes. It is perfectly true that I should like to have the purse (and sheer digestive capacity) to eat as well – and as often – as Mr Mayle, and survive. Even more, I should like to make as much money as he does by writing such slim, superficial books about an area I have lived in, off and on, since 1960, which consist of little more than lists of expensive restaurant menus and provencal antiques and food markets.

Well, I may have got there first in time, but it appears that Peter Mayle got to a publisher first and so good luck to him. He gives himself away rather badly in the new book by describing the parking area next to a posh restaurant as looking 'as though the local Porsche and Mercedes dealers are having a convention; cell phones, titanium-framed sunglasses and Vuitton beach bags litter the tables.' This, though he would deny it, is basically the world Mr Mayle, an ex-advertising man, loves. I had hoped to reach the end of this piece without using the word 'vulgar', but it is inevitable. What Mr Mayle has achieved with his books is to turn beautiful, ancient Provence into just another international 'product', one now visited by coach-loads of camera-strung Japanese who constitute his readers.

It so happens that I am writing this in Avignon during the annual festival of music and drama, which is one of the things Mr Mayle recommends to his readers, along with riding a bicycle up Mont Ventoux and running naked through the Luberon. The festival, with no less than 550 separate spectacles, is now a lot of old tat, a classic illustration of Kingsley Amis's adage that 'more means worse'. Forty years ago, when it was just a couple of plays and a concert, it as well worth attending, but the plays it now puts on are so boring and the people presenting them so avaricious that one longs to escape the over-loaded oven that is Avignon in July to the cool hinterland of Provence, assuming one can find a quiet corner now that Mr Mayle has re-invaded it.

To be scrupulously fair, which I always try to be, Peter Mayle in lyrical mode can write as well as anybody: 'Later that day, I took the dogs for a walk on the plateau of Le Clapare above Bonnieux. It was early evening, and over the mountains to the east a three-quarter moon was rising, pale and milky against the blue sky, balanced by the sun falling in the west. The air was warm and dry, sharp with the scent of the sariette that grows wild in pockets of earth between the rocks. The only sound was the wind, the only visible souvenir of man's presence a few yards of collapsed drystone wall lumped among the bushes. The view could hardly have changed in hundreds of years, perhaps thousands, and it was a reminder of the quick blink of time that represents a human life.'

I have lived in, or around, Bonnieux for many a summer, and write about it, but I never produced a paragraph half as good as that. Sour grapes again.

Pope Goes the Weasel

I was received into the Roman Catholic Church by the Dominicans at Blackfriars, Oxford, on 28 October 1979. Assuming I am not first arrested for breach of probation, I propose to celebrate this anniversary by making a pilgrimage to the Shrine of Our Lady at Walsingham. The Norfolk police are welcome to pick me up there, if they want to. (I have been in their hands before and they treated me rather well.)

I am a daily Mass-goer in England and France. Allowing for the odd day missed, but taking into account Sundays when I sometimes go twice, that makes about 7,000 times I have taken the Blessed Sacrament over two decades. Has it done me any good?

The answer has to be a qualified no. I quite often find that my troubled spirit is soothed by attending Mass, and the day goes better as a result. There have been a very few occasions (at Ealing Abbey in London, for some reason, and once or twice in France) when I have experienced a positive accretion of strength, but that is about it. Most of the time it leaves me bored and indifferent. I am reminded of a remark of Evelyn Waugh's, in his diaries, that all his Catholic faith does for him is to turn his savage indignation against the world into massive boredom. I identify with that. I also identify with his words to Nancy Mitford, when she upbraided him for being abusively rude to a poor American woman at her lunch table: 'What you don't understand, Nancy, is that if I weren't a Catholic I'd be even worse.'

My parents, before they died, expressed the view that

conversion to Catholicism had done nothing to improve my character. I think they must have been right about that, since I have spent nearly half of these 20 years under various forms of legal restraint – bail, probation, prison – for diverse fiscal offences. I think they would have agreed with the senior screw in HMP Exeter (1993) when he asked me, 'If you're so ****ing religious,' – expletive deleted – 'then what the **** are you doing in here?' (Further expletive deleted.)

The answer to that, though it appears complicated, is actually quite simple. Catholic spirituality, like other forms of spirituality, has no moral content per se. It is morally neutral. It is perfectly possible to be a bad person and remain deeply religious. I always cite the (admittedly rather corny) example of Rasputin, who was a thoroughly filthy fellow, a womaniser and a drunk, but possessed remarkable spiritual powers which he used to heal, among others, the heir to the Russian throne. I, too, am a bad person, yet I believe myself to be a spiritual one. And I have a deep need for religion.

The Roman Catholic Church in Britain I have found to be an unmitigated disaster: snobbish, venal, hypocritical and deeply philistine. I could number on the fingers of one hand the parish priests I have met who have struck me as doing their job properly, and as for the hierarchy, well, the ridiculous fuss over Cardinal Hume's recent demise is a case in point. Hume was a force for good in the world, no doubt about that, but in private he was also a vain, irascible, petulant man with a very quick temper. How absurd of William Rees-Mogg to suggest in the *Times* that he should be numbered among the few British saints. However, to be fair to Basil Hume, he was honest enough to admit – again in private – that the spiritual journey is generally one into greater darkness than into the light.

Here in France, the Catholic Church sits more easily – it is a Catholic country, after all – but for sheer money-grabbing greed and venality it leaves even the English Church far behind. Two collections plus a retiring one are the norm at Sunday Mass and, speaking as an almost destitute person, I am sick to death of having to pretend to put money in the plate when I really feel like taking money out of it.

So why do I choose to remain a member of a Church I despise? I can provide three reasons. Firstly, I became a Catholic in order to save my soul. It would be pointless to apostatise now after 20 years, thus jeopardising the prospect of salvation. (I am attached to the concept of the immortal soul but not to Catholic notions of heaven and hell, which strike me as mediaeval. In fact, I have never understood why belief in God predicates belief in a life after death. I think we make our own heaven and hell here on earth. I agree with my old friend Lord Melvyn Bragg, when he asked God, in a recent *Independent* interview, 'Why do I only get one shot at this?')

Secondly, attending Mass every morning is a very good discipline. I use the time, not necessarily to pray, but to reflect on my life and those of my few friends and many enemies. I sometimes use it to compose in my mind whichever article I am currently working on. I used to hate getting up early, indeed getting up at all, but going to Mass every day has changed that. I now positively look forward to it.

Thirdly – and this is the weird bit – I have developed an extraordinary devotion to Our Blessed Lady, as I explained in a review of a book about Lourdes in *Oldie* 123. She has seen me through so many incredibly difficult times that it would be dishonest, ungrateful, and downright illogical to desert Her now. Of course, all this may be no worse than a devotion to the female principle in life, and in myself, but that doesn't matter. It is rather like falling in love. One doesn't expect it to happen but, when it does, it is best and wisest to go along with it...

Maugham wrote in *The Moon and Sixpence* that there are

men whose desire for truth is so great that, to attain it, they will shatter the very foundations of their world. I suppose I may now number myself among them. If so, I have no regrets.

What Did You Do in the War, Papie?

Early in the 1990s I lived for a while with an elderly, old-fashioned extended French family in the small town of Dol, just south of St Malo in Brittany. They were in the dry-cleaning business but also owned a large house which they used to let rooms at very low rents to artists and impoverished writers. We all became very friendly over the months – one of the spinster daughters had a crush on me – and I was even invited to join them for Sunday lunch, an almost unheard-of compliment from the normally inhospitable French. At one such lunch – in their beautiful garden, as I recall – during the autumn of 1991, conversation turned to the Second World War, and I heard myself asking what turned out to be a fateful question: 'And how did you all get on in the war?'

The response to this innocent enquiry was both dramatic and catastrophic. Knives and forks remained suspended between plate and mouth; wine glasses were left untouched. There was a long and terrible silence. Finally, the *père de famille* roused himself to reply to my question by asking one himself: 'And why exactly,' he asked in a strangulated voice, 'do you wish to know?'

Things were never the same after that. No more invitations to lunch. My rent was put up. A few weeks later, crawling towards Dol railway station laden with baggage and typewriter, it suddenly came to me that they must have thought I suspected them of having collaborated during the war. Perhaps they thought I had been sent to spy on them. Perhaps they *had* collaborated. What did it matter anyhow?

To the French it still, of course, matters a great deal. The memories and scars of the Second World War, which ended over half a century ago, are still as fresh in France as though it ended yesterday. You either collaborated or you resisted. There is no grey area in between. (It is interesting, in this connection, that researchers for the famous film about life during the Occupation in the city of Clermont Ferrand, *The Sorrow and the Pity*, came up with the statistic that 50 per cent of the inhabitants collaborated and 50 per cent resisted.)

The French obsession with the Second World War is something I can never get used to. Channel-switching in French hotel rooms in search of something worth watching, as is my wont, I have yet to pass an evening without chancing upon a TV programme devoted to some aspect of it, normally to the shameful Vichy episode. If I have seen poor old Marshal Pétain in the dock once, I have seen him a thousand times. The tongue returns to the aching tooth...

The psychology behind all this is complicated. The French feel guilty about Vichy, of course, and about the activities of *fonctionnaires* like Maurice Papon, who sent hundred of Jews to their deaths. Mingled with this feeling of guilt is a deep reluctance to feel grateful to anybody, least of all to the British, for helping them out during the war. This accounts for the strangely ambivalent attitude that I, as an Englishman living in France, have been at the receiving end of for the past nine years. Gratitude is a complex emotion: none of us, in his heart of hearts, enjoys feeling a debt of gratitude to anybody else. (The uneasy relations between de Gaulle and Churchill in wartime perfectly illustrated this).

Not far from Limoges, where I'm now living, is the 'martyr'

village of Oradour-sur-Glane, where 642 French men, women and children were slaughtered by the Nazis on 10 June 1944. Today, no birds sing there. The French attitude towards the Germans, their recent enemy (we, the British, are their ancient enemy), is even more complicated.

A few years ago, under Kohl-Mitterrand, who got on well, it really seemed that a genuine *entente* was taking place. But now, under Chirac-Schröder, who get on less well, the relationship has cooled. I come upon little pockets of anti-German feeling and resentment almost every day. Because, despite being British, I look rather Teutonic (my mother was German), I am sometimes at the receiving end of that as well ...

A few weeks ago, I was staying in a rather terrible *foyer* in Caen, full of tramps and drunks and juvenile delinquents. Three young gorillas got it into their heads that I was German and took to singing out 'Heil Hitler' and making the Nazi salute whenever they passed me in the passage. I got fed up with this after a few days and finally retaliated with a salute of my own devising. Whereupon they followed me into my room and – there is no polite way of saying this – beat the living shit out of me.

There was something very French about this incident. They can dish it out, but they can't take it. This is commonly known as cowardice. Since I am British but look German, I am currently getting the worst of both worlds over here. I am not sure that I can take it for much longer.

On 11 November, a public holiday in France, elaborate, solemn and vainglorious ceremonies will once again mark the ending of the war to end war. But they will never get it right. Parachutists will descend from the skies towards city squares and end up entangled in neighbouring buildings (I actually saw this happen in Toulouse). Soldiers will faint on parade; horses will defecate. Colonels in kepis will stand at attention with cigarettes between their fingers. It will all be very untidy. It is something we have always done better than the French and always will do better. Perhaps they should try to forget about the war for a generation or two and concentrate on living in the present.

Walsingham Attila

I should not wish to depress or upset *Oldie* readers by describing the Cambridge hostel for the homeless I am currently living in. Suffice to say that it is known as the hostel from hell. Suffice to say, too, that, on my fourth morning here, a tattooed thug in the room next door loosened six of my teeth when I complained about the volume of his 'music'. Two of these needed extraction anyway, so I suppose I should be grateful to him, but it didn't feel like that at the time. (The scum is 'looking at' two years for assaulting a policeman: I told him he could make that seven if I decided to press charges for GBH on an OAP.)

The only thing was to escape on pilgrimage to Walsingham to celebrate 20 years as a Roman Catholic. The train to Kings Lynn got in late, so I missed the connecting bus to Fakenham and decided to lunch modestly on soup and a roll at the unprepossessing bus station while a number of buses marked SORRY, I'M NOT IN SERVICE rolled past. (A youth behind me in the queue was told he would have to wait a while for his coffee because they had a 'rush' on. The rush turned out to be my soup and roll.)

When I finally found another bus, the driver's mini ticket computer had broken down. He didn't have any change. He didn't even know the route. When he consulted me, I told him I had never been to this part of Norfolk in my life. At Fakenham, a number of other buses marked SORRY, I'M NOT IN SERVICE whizzed past. With the resolution born of despair, I hijacked one and demanded of the surly driver that he take me to Walsingham, 'England's Nazareth.' Rather surprisingly, he agreed. It is amazing what a certain amount of willpower (or prayer) can achieve.

Arriving at the holy village, I booked into the Sue Ryder ecumenical bed-and-breakfast (£18 per night), which seemed to be full of twittering spinsters and elderly widows. I had no sooner taken to my bed to recover from the assault course on my sensibilities occasioned by the vagaries of the Norfolk public transport system, when one of these, upper-class-sounding, tapped on my door wanting to know if I needed a spare table-lamp. I told her, in language reminiscent of the hostel from hell, to shove off. (Given the choice between living among tattooed gorillas and these twittering *soi-disant* ecumenical ladies I'm not sure I don't prefer the former.)

She sounded rather shocked. She got her revenge, however, On my way to the bathroom, clad only in a pair of (stolen) BHS green underpants, I managed to lock myself out of my bedroom and was obliged to seek out, soap and flannel in hand, the spinsters' common room to get the master key. The twittering ceased abruptly, then noticeably increased in volume at the sight of my almost naked torso. I apologised profusely for my earlier profanity – but to the wrong woman. (I never did find out whom I had actually sworn at.)

My policy when things are going so badly wrong as this is to take refuge in the flesh. It is the flesh that saves us when the spirit fails – and one can have too much religion, after all. By flesh, I mean eating, drinking and sex. There did not seem much likelihood of finding sex in Walsingham on a weekend in late October, but I drifted down to the Bull Hotel and drank two pints of lager and made an excellent meal of prawn cocktail, beef with abundant vegetables, and apple pie, all washed down with a very drinkable claret, for £30, including a generous gratuity. That represents, for me, four days Old King Cole (dole) money – and it's worth every penny.

Next morning I found myself with time on my hands, so wandered down to the rather gloomy Anglican shrine with a number of pilgrims from a parish near Birmingham who were praying that the trapped nerve in Edna's spine might soon be freed and that Sid might pass his HGV driving test. The parson in charge had one of those braying Anglican voices that sound as though, while preaching, he is trying to move a thin strip of india rubber glued to the roof of his mouth, using only his tongue. I left their Mass pretty promptly, I can tell you, and went back to breakfast with the spinsters.

Later, it turned sunny, so after a visit to the Orthodox Chapel I strolled through the fields to the Roman Catholic shrine, where a barmy old woman with dyed red hair and foul breath seized me by the arm, Ancient Mariner fashion, and harangued me with the Walsingham legend, which I knew anyway. One of the troubles with the RC Church in Britain is that there are too many deranged people like this in it. I managed to escape her clutches and went into the extremely vulgar, philistine new church where a number of rather slimy priests were celebrating All Saints to a small congregation by no means sound in wind and limb. At Walsingham, the disabled are, if anything, over-catered for. I am aware that there is a huge disabled subculture in this country (two million at a recent estimate), but it is reaching the point where, if you are able-bodied, you feel left out.

After the beauty and simplicity of Lourdes, Walsingham struck me as low and mean and second-rate. I know that I shall be condemned as a hopeless intellectual and social snob for saying so but – with the single exception of the unseen spinster who tapped on my door – I met no one of culture or refinement the entire weekend. Everybody was common and ugly and working-class. Of course, I accept that Catholicism has evolved as a religion to suit the masses and was not designed for an intense individualist, but all the same… The other disappointment was that there was no real devotion to Our Blessed Lady that I could discern. There were repeated prayers that She return to reclaim England as Her rightful dowry (an unlikely prospect, whichever way you look at it), but no feeling of spiritual dedication to Her.

I will not describe to you the bus journey back to Cambridge and its hostel from hell because, quite simply, you would not believe me. Suffice to say that I was not expecting to see the Christmas decorations at Wells-next-the-Sea, but now I have. I have, however, achieved one thing – the Walsingham visit has supplied me with a title for my memoirs for which I have been thrashing around for many months: SORRY, I'M NOT IN SERVICE. That is exactly how I feel about life as the century turns.

Cambridge Blues

The Cambridge 'hostel from hell' where I'm currently living is packed with people who have just come out of prison or are about to go back in. I ought to feel at home among them, but I don't. After being beaten up by tattooed thugs, as described last month, I was moved into the 'yellow' section of the hostel. If I may quote from something I wrote for their newsletter:

'The "yellow" section is the OAP wing. We old men take life pretty easy over here. We do not see each other for days on end. We are like fishes swimming in a deep pool, who rarely bump into each other. Very occasionally, we cook a meal together or watch the telly, but the rest of the time we keep ourselves to ourselves. Occasionally, I might pick a resident's brain for help in solving my crossword puzzle, or I might ask if I may have a spoonful of their Nesquick. But that is about it. Minimal contact of this kind suits me down to the ground, since I have no wish to "bond" with my fellow residents – although I have nothing against them. I try to be polite and friendly with everybody I meet, so if there is any hassle, it is the other person's fault, not mine...'

All this was too good to last, of course. Returning from pilgrimage to Walsingham, I was moved into a brutal modern house at the far end of the hostel compound, presided over by a deeply paranoid, alcoholic ex-college chef who uses his pathological obesity to bully and psychologically manipulate those around him. In me he has found someone he can't manipulate, which makes him angrier than ever. (I am still with him as I write and hating every moment of it.)

I tried to escape from these dismal crooks into Cambridge

university circles, but I didn't fare much better there. Little St Mary, the church attached to Peterhouse, announced the 'Archbishop Michael Ramsey' lecture, and I thought I would go along since I was, briefly, press secretary to the old boy in the early 1970s. The subject was 'Evidence for the Resurrection' and the lecturer a dusty old professor, wearing a shabby, 1950s brown suit and a short-sleeved knitted pullover, straight from central casting. He made a ludicrous attempt to prove the Resurrection mathematically – an absurdity almost beyond belief, I thought. Still, it's good to know that the old Cambridge pastime of trying to prove the unprovable is still alive and well. This event could have taken place at almost any time in the past 200 years. It bore no relevance to my life – I don't believe in the Resurrection anyway – or to the life of anybody else in the audience, so far as I could see.

So Bill Cave, chaplain aboard HMP Weare in 1998, was right when he told me that if I couldn't settle in Cambridge I couldn't settle anywhere. The city seems to be divided between the criminal/homeless fraternity, with whom – despite appearances – I have very little in common, and the snobbish, self-regarding university, with whom I have even less. All this may be symbolically summed up by my daily attendance at Mass at the University Catholic Chaplaincy whose sanctity is invariably disturbed by the young beggars shouting 'Big Issue!' in the street outside the chapel. The smug, mealy-mouthed priests don't have the guts to tell them to shut up; and it would certainly never occur to these aggressive tramps that they were disturbing the meditations of would-be saints like myself. A plague on both their houses…'

I tried to escape yet again by going up to Liverpool to see my new granddaughter, Hope. On this subject, idealising one's children and grandchildren, Raymond Briggs said something so perceptive in *Oldie* 120 in the course of an interview with Naim Attallah, that I quote it in full:

'I just feel that when people have a new baby, things are absolutely wonderful, as of course they are, but then it seems to me that as time goes on things become less and less wonderful. The huge event is the birth, it's supremely miraculous that this amazing creature has appeared from nowhere, and then they become more and more pedestrian the older they get. By the time they're teenagers they've become fairly insufferable, and then when they grow out of that stage they become quite ordinary, like the people next door. So there's a slight anti-climax to the whole thing; you might still love them, of course, but they've become fairly ordinary.'

To which Attallah responds: 'But don't you think we idealise our children because they contain the future, they are symbols of hope. They might not turn out as we hope but if we stop hoping, is that not worse?'

This interesting exchange was running through my mind as I made the extremely tiresome coach journey across wrecked England from Cambridge to Liverpool via Milton Keynes. National Express likes to advertise its efficiency, but the Milton Keynes coach came in marked 'Oxford' and the Liverpool coach was marked 'Southport', so l nearly missed them both. Pondering on this as we hung around in the gloom of the St Neots industrial estate and Tesco Centre and the Milton Keynes Coachway (existential wildernesses in the middle of nowhere), I began to understand why people feel a sense of oppression and despair at the thought of the new century, which hangs over them like a black cloud, bearing with it the debris of the horrifying century just past. They know, too, that it is the century they will die in, which adds to their depression.

These Millennium blues were banished by a glimpse of my first grandchild's sweet little face. Here, fast asleep in her carry-cot, was Hope writ large. The sight of her was sufficient to enable me to endure the rigours of the return journey – the Birmingham coach wasn't marked at all; there was a bomb scare at Digbeth coach station; the Cambridge coach featured a driver of unbelievable surliness – with equanimity. Perhaps there is hope, after all.

Food, Glorious Food

For the first time in living memory, I arrived in France with a bit of money in my pocket. Not very much, I hasten to add – about 700 francs (£70) – but enough for a quiet hotel in Avignon and my favourite French menu: salade niçoise, escaloppe Milanaise, pêche melba. As I paid the restaurant bill of 158 francs (about £15) it occurred to me that I could have enjoyed the same meal, if not better, for nothing at Visa *foyer*, my next destination…

Watching the sad procession of vagrants, alcoholics and psychotics trooping through the Visa gate the next evening, I already began to feel guilty for having deserted them for even one night. *Foyer* life is psychologically exhausting but at the same time curiously addictive. The wizened, prematurely aged faces of my fellow residents, their filthy clothes and foul smell can soon become familiar, even endearing. The French have a phrase for this: *nostalgie de la boue*.

Roland, the highly progressive, defiantly pro-British young director of Visa, and his English-speaking deputy Patrick were anxious to show off their Christmas and New Year food arrangements for the SDF (Sans Domicile Fire, i.e. homeless), and I, of course, was only too anxious to sample them. They employ a talented young chef, Olivier, who once ran a brilliant restaurant and will probably do so again one day. He cooks up a superb lunch every weekday for five francs for anyone who cares to drop in, and an equally superb (free) evening meal for the permanent residents. For Christmas Eve, Olivier offered us *terrine de chevreuil et sa salade, faux filet de boeuf aux ceps, assortiment de légumes, fromage, Gâteau de Noël* (basically, pâté, roast beef, vegetables, cheese,

Christmas cake), accompanied by no fewer than four wines: one white, two red, and champagne. All '*gratuit*', naturally, courtesy of the French state. Merci, M. Chirac!

I was almost put off my Christmas dinner by a disgusting old Arab defecating in his bedroom, all down the *foyer* corridor and all over our bathroom. '*Pas grave. On nettoye*' – 'It doesn't matter. It'll be cleaned up' – was all he had to say when we remonstrated with him. A selfish enough attitude but also a realistic one since Visa has 15 staff members (about one per two residents) standing by to do just that.

'*L' enfer, C'est les autres*,' said Sartre – hell is other people. Last July, in the Avignon *foyer*, I bought a pathetic old tramp, Jean-Luc, a couple of beers for no other reason than that I felt sorry for him. Now Jean-Luc's fortunes have suddenly changed for the better, his ship has come home (against the normal run of the mill for the SDF, 90 per cent of whom sink deeper and deeper into degradation) and he has been showering me with beers, wine, whisky, lunches. He has even lent me a bit of money. Cynical *Oldie* readers will say that I only treated him to the beers as an investment for future scrounging, but this is not, in fact, the case. I am reminded of something I have noticed ever since I started living the French *foyers* in 1992: it is, invariably, the poor who give to one, not the rich. For New Year, Olivier excelled himself again: *fuilleté de poisson/sauce homardine, faux filet bearnaise, pommes paillasses, tomates provençales, fromage, Déssert 2000* (fish with lobster sauce, roast beef, vegetable cheese, and the sweet which was like ambrosia), accompanied again, by three wines, including an excellent Bordeaux, and more champagne.

I sat with Patrick, the English-speaking *sous-directeur*, and after congratulating him on the food, made the only New Year's resolution that I have ever been known to make, namely that I am going to plunge ever more deeply into French *foyer* life in this year 2000, and so I have already made plans for Limoges (La Bonne

Assiette) and Saumur (La Table Ouverte) – names of what the French call *restaurants sociaux*, where one eats well and for nothing – La Roche-sur-Yon and La Rochelle for the coming months.

Examining this list, I am forced to admit to myself that the main motive for my choice is food, glorious food. The late Arthur Marshall remarked to me once that enjoyment of good food was the one consolation of old age as all the other senses, particularly those related to sex, atrophy and die. It is true that the taste buds, too, are dying off at the rate of several million per day, but I still have many billions in reserve and I intend to go on expending them in the wonderful French *foyers* for just as long as I can.

Fiddler on the Rails

Sometimes, during the long, sleepless nights that are so much a part of my life in the French *foyers*, I lie listening to the shunting of the goods trains in the freight yards and the passing roar of the Paris Express and imagine myself as the eponymous hero of Simenon's *The Man Who Watched the Trains Go By*. Then, in the mornings, I wake up to reality (*Bonjour Tristesse!*) and have to face the fact that I am not the man who watched the trains go by. I am simply the man who travels free on the SNCF...

I have been jumping the French trains for six years now. (Only yesterday, I travelled from Limoges to Saumur via Vierzon and Tours, a four-hour journey involving three expresses, and it cost me not a sou, though a good deal in nervous exhaustion.) Expelled from Lourdes by the police in December 1993 for 'doing' two hotels and two convents, I was obliged to explain myself as best I could – I had no money – to the *controlleur* on the Toulouse express. To my surprise, he took it very calmly, merely glanced at my passport and issued a little yellow slip, known as an *avis d'infraction*, to cover my journey. (The theory is that a bill for the fare plus a hefty fine is sent on to your home address at a later date.)

Since then, I have been issued with about 200 *avis d'infraction*, covering the entire length and breadth of *la belle France*. At an average of, say 100 francs each, that makes 20,000 francs (about £2,000) I owe the SNCF. They throw you off trains right away in Germany, Italy and Spain, but I have been thrown off a French train only once. That was in the Pyrenees in 1996, when I foolishly and arrogantly sat in first-class and expected to travel for nothing from Pau to Bayonne. The *controlleur* made me get off at Orthez in the middle of nowhere, but I kept my cool and simply sat and waited for the next train, on which there was no 'control' at all…

My original policy was to sit in second-class and wait for the controlleur to come round, then explain to him that I had no money, which was usually the truth. Occasionally, I would embroider this a trifle by saying that I had been robbed on a cross-Channel ferry or in a *foyer* – sometimes true, too. Recently, however, they have been tightening up and demanding a home address in France as well as in England, from where they have great difficulty in collecting the money due. (Not that I have ever received a bill in either.)

So now I have evolved a new policy to take account of the fact that the *controlleur* may cut up rough. I examine him (or her) very carefully to see if he looks the type that might turn awkward. (I possess a highly developed instinct for this kind of thing.) If he looks OK, then I simply wait for him to come round. If he looks disagreeable, then I summon up the nerve to approach him first with my trumped-up story of having just been robbed of all my cash. This rarely fails, since the soft-hearted French are invariably pleased and flattered at being asked for help by a foreigner in distress.

Best of all are the small local trains, which carry only one *controlleur*, and he is too busy shouting out the names of the country stations to have time to check the tickets. So you are able to travel for free – and without anxiety.

Hardest are the *controlleurs* on the TGV (*trains de grande vitesse*) trains going down to Marseilles from Paris. They are usually extremely arrogant, well-paid Arabs with an intense dislike for 'dishonest' white persons like myself. On a recent trip to Avignon, I watched one of them throw off a young man (Arab, actually) before we had even left the Gare de Lyon. He was extremely suspicious of my tale of having been robbed on the ferry ('Why didn't they take your passport as well?' he asked, reasonably enough) and was about to phone through to the SNCF police when he was distracted by an extremely beautiful young blonde (when French blondes are beautiful they are really beautiful) coming to sit, by mistake, in his own reserved first-class compartment. By the time he had finished 'flirting' with her (an understatement – he practically seduced her on the luxury seat) we were drawing into the Avignon suburbs and I was able to hop off the train scot-free – yet again.

It is always fatal to boast. I was about to put this account of how to jump the French trains into the post when a nasty-looking official document was delivered to me by hand at the *foyer* in Limoges. It was from the legal department of the SNCF regarding an unpaid first-class fare (600 francs) for a journey from Limoges to Paris I made last September. It requires me to pay the money at once, failing which – a massive fine or even imprisonment.

It looks as though the SNCF computers have caught up with me at last. Well, it's a fair cop and I have had a good railway run for my (lack of) money. I shall go down with all my guns blazing and then I shall start jumping the French trains all over again.

Four Foyer Friends

Not all the Frenchmen who do the rounds of the *foyers* are tramps, drunks or hopeless neurotics. Some of them are quite sane. And intelligent. Some have even become my friends...

Jean, 65, is known on the *foyer* circuit as 'the Professor', because of a didactic way of speaking. He was once a director of a large oil company. He has worked in America and Canada and understands English. The loss of his wife and children (in a car crash) would seem to have traumatised him for, since then, he has lived exclusively in the *foyers*. A handsome man, whom all the *foyer* waitresses and cleaners adore, Jean is, in fact, a professional gambler. He once sold me his umbrella for 20 francs (£2) and put the money on a horse that came in at l00–l. Jean spent the 2,000 francs on a luxury hotel room and a rich meal – quite an easy thing to do in Toulouse – and was back in the foyer the following night.

He says he will retire to an apartment in Cahors one day, but I doubt this. I doubt, too, whether he has a father, aged 92, still living in Alsace, who will one day leave Jean all his fortune. The fact is, Jean just enjoys living in *foyers*. He is extremely well-read and knows his way round the European political scene. He lectures me occasionally, in his slightly patronising way, on British politics, about which he knows more than I do. He pays me the compliment of saying that I am the only serious Englishman he has ever met.

Gerard, 50, is another *foyer* friend, based in Angers, but constantly on the move: Saumur, Tarbes, Vierzon, Toulouse, Orleans, etc. He spends all his days in various municipal libraries reading about the Third Reich, and he knows more about Adolf

Hitler than Adolf can have known about himself. Not that Gerard has any fascist tendencies – he is horrified by recent events in Austria and is a genuine French socialist and republican who believes that Britain will not progress unless she gets rid of her royal family. Gérard is the kind of man who would share his last meal with you and can always be relied on for a loan. The only thing that upsets him is when I ask him if he is *au chômage*, i.e. out of work. 'I do not believe in work,' he says with dignity, and has never worked in his life. He has no family. I have met many social outcasts in the French *foyers*, but Gérard is the real thing. He says he will commit suicide when he reaches 65.

I have made many friends among the *foyer* staff as well. Michel, the director of the one in Limoges, with his ugly, broken, ex-boxer's nose and his immensely caring attitude towards even his most difficult clients, is almost certainly homosexual. I have to admit that he brings out vague homosexual inclinations in myself, though that may be no more than one of the symptoms of paranoia from which I suffer, all part of the increasing narcissism of old age.

One of Michel's most demanding clients is not a man at all. Aida, the *foyer* tart, has lived there for seven years. She was expelled from Morocco after serving two years for a *crime passionel*. At the *foyer*, she has been known to give *pipe* (fellatio) for as little at 20 francs (£2). She is always immensely kind to me: indeed, we have struck up a weird kind of friendship. Whenever I am really short of money, which is most of the time, she goes off to the Gare des Benedictins (the Limoges station) for a couple of hours and returns with a fistful of 200-franc notes for me. What she does to obtain these I have no idea. (Michel once told me that she specialises in sex for the handicapped – whatever it is, it must be extremely well paid.) Yet Aida is old and ugly. It is a mystery I prefer not to penetrate. (I cannot even admit to myself that I am living off the earnings of prostitution.)

The one thing I really cannot bear is to encounter other

Englishmen in the French *foyers*. There was a certain (homosexual) ex-public school boy, a former head boy of Dulwich College, who had drifted into alcoholism, at the *foyer* in Toulouse. He was one of the most atrocious people I have ever met, though he spoke superb French. Only recently in Limoges I met a young tramp from Fleet, Hampshire, of all places. I didn't like him either. I suppose what I really detest in these people is the mirror image of myself. One never knows who is going to turn up next. An *Oldie* subscriber?

Some Day I'll Find You

There is a terrible joke doing the rounds in France which has Clinton and the Pope both dying on the same day. Due to bureaucratic confusion on St Peter's part, the Pope is sent to Hell and Clinton to Heaven. The muddle is sorted out within 24 hours and the two pass each other en route to their rightful destination. 'Bill, I'm so sorry,' says the ascending John Paul II, 'but, at last, I shall see the Blessed Virgin!' 'I'm sorry too,' says Clinton laconically, 'because you're too late…'

The best bit of this joke, for me, is 'at last, I shall see the Blessed Virgin!' because that is what I have been trying to do for some years now. A small, balding man named Serge who goes to the same church as myself in Limoges finally persuaded me that She appears at monthly intervals in an Italian hamlet named San Damiano, just south of Milan, so – not without a certain reluctance – I decided to accompany him and about 3,000 others on a May pilgrimage in the hope of seeing Her at last.

The big day began with a six-hour drive eastwards to Clermont-Ferrand – by no means my favourite French city ever since I read the statistic that 50 per cent of its inhabitants collaborated with the Nazis during the Second World War. As we entered the suburbs, I rather tactlessly announced this fact to my French fellow-passengers, and they all went rather quiet. In fact, they didn't speak to me again for several hours…

At St Etienne we were joined on the coach by the pilgrimage boss, a retired barber named Raymond, the type of French *commerçant* I particularly dislike since he seemed to be devoting his commercial instincts to exploiting us poor, superstitious Catholics. The actual cost of the trip had been announced as 600 francs (£60) but a number of hidden 'extras' emerged as the long day wore on: membership of his pilgrimage 'club', 70 francs (£7); extra petrol, 60 francs (£6); prayer books, 40 francs (£4); holy oil, 60 francs; breakfast, 30 francs – this rose to 50 francs when I asked for a second cup of coffee; Masses for the dead, 40 francs; coach driver's tip, 50 francs. I could go on and on, but you get the general idea. It soon became clear that the weekend was going to cost me £100, and rising. With 50 passengers to fill his coach, the barber was not going to do too badly out of it. No wonder he was smiling and rubbing his hands as he said his Rosary. This was the money-grabbing French as their worst, I thought.

San Damiano has one thing in common with Lourdes and one thing in stark contrast. The thing it has in common is a very beautiful natural situation (despite the proximity of a NATO air base which was used in the Kosovo war) in the valley of the Po, just south of the fine city of Piacenza. The thing it doesn't have in common is a total failure to separate 'shrine' from 'shopping', as they have done so successfully at Lourdes.

I was extremely tired and thirsty when we arrived (18 hours of travel by car and coach can do that to you). So at once I went in search of the holy spring, whose water was the coolest and sweetest I have ever tasted – just like a very light Italian wine. Also there was a wonderful scent of roses (made to bloom by Our Lady Herself, if the legend is to be believed) and of the rich, ripe Lombardy countryside. After drinking the holy water, I fell into a deep, refreshing sleep on a handy bench just in front of a pure white statue of the Blessed Virgin and woke, two hours later, to find a beautiful black girl sitting next to me.

Just for a moment, I thought my Jamaican friends must be right when they said that Our Lady was black, not white. But she had a rather plain friend with her, and I realised that she was just another pilgrim – one of about 400 coachloads, since I had chosen the 30th anniversary of the first apparition (to Mamma Rosa, an illiterate Italian peasant) to make my pilgrimage to San Damiano in search of the Blessed Virgin.

They have, as I say, failed to separate shrine and shopping there. It is the old, old story of one set of credulous peasants being ripped off by another set of commercial ones. The extra 20 francs for a cup of coffee was the last straw as far as I was concerned. After the Rosary (at 5 am!) and Mass said by six priests (8.30 am), I returned to the pilgrimage coach to assemble my scattered thoughts. A horrible thick cloud, typical of the Po Valley, had descended on San Damiano, and there appeared very little prospect of seeing Our Lady that day. The other pilgrims kept assuring me that the clouds would soon break and that we should see the Blessed Virgin descending in all Her glory (Serge had previously shown me some remarkable photographs, apparently unfaked, of her doing just that), but I knew, in my heart of hearts, that the cloud and fog had set in for the day.

It was disappointing, but it seemed to me that what I was really looking for in making this pilgrimage was the presence of some kind of ideal female in my life. I found her, a few minutes later, in the person of the beautiful black girl, whom I ran into again for a short while, and who made a very acceptable substitute for the Blessed Virgin (Adventures of the Black Girl in Search of God?). Either that or, as I suggested in an *Oldie* piece last year, the whole thing may be no more than a response to the feminine side of myself, of which I have become increasingly aware as the years have rolled by.

I do not despair. I still believe She is out there somewhere, hiding away behind the dark clouds lowering over the Po Valley.

One day I shall see her for myself. That knowledge made the horrible return journey, the relentless, vain repetition of the Rosary and the equally relentless commercial onslaught just a little more acceptable.

Alsatian Whine

I am sorry to report that I have slipped back into my bad old ways: staying at hotels and not paying the bill. This, however, was not recidivism but a press tour of Alsace sponsored by Inntravel, an organisation which encourages old people to travel independently. The train journey up from Avignon, where I was staying in Visa *foyer*, to Strasbourg took forever (eight hours) – I jumped it, as usual – and I was so tired that I broke one of my own rules and flagged an expensive taxi for the short walk to the Cathedral Hotel, where an indifferent girl receptionist came off her mobile long enough to tell me that Mass next morning was at 8 am. In fact, it was at 7 so I missed it. *Ça commence bien.* A good start…

The press party arrived weary and dishevelled at Entzheim, the Strasbourg airport, having assembled at the Gatwick south terminal when the plane took off from the north one. They drifted through gate one while their baggage arrived in bits and pieces on the carousel at gate two. I thought of the oldie airline joke: breakfast in London, lunch in Paris, luggage in Istanbul - and was glad to note that air travel has scarcely changed since my own jet-setting heyday. It is just as horrible as ever. *Ça commence encore plus bien…*

My fellow journalists were so ghastly that I prefer not to describe them. In fact, I promise not to mention them again and you must imagine that I made this strange journey on my own. The cliché is that Alsace is a region of France where the houses and village names (Kaysersberg, Kientzheim, etc – they all seem to begin with K) reflect the proximity of Germany, just across the Rhine, but where the people remain passionately French. In fact, it is more complicated than that. Most of the people look and behave extremely Teutonically. The hotels we stayed in en route – the worst, incidentally, I have ever been to; it would be demeaning even to jump them – all seemed to be run by large, leathery, humourless, bossy blonde women who looked as though they should have been wearing Tyrolean hats and shorts in place of the insipid Alsatian costume which made them look like Morris dancers, probably the unsexiest dress (or dance) ever devised by humankind. Meanwhile, their luckless husbands and sons stood cowering at the corners of the hotel reception areas, awaiting orders. Alsace is a matriarchy.

It is also a gloomy region at the best of times, reflecting perhaps the many attritional wars that have been fought over it across the centuries – the most characteristic thing we came upon during our walks through the Vosges hills was a perfectly preserved (German) bunker, dating from the First World War – and not helped very much by the incessant rainfall that deluged the whole of France during May. The area reminds one of Central Europe – Transylvania, perhaps – with storks nesting on the roofs of half-timbered houses that look as though they have been constructed by a clumsy child with a large fretsaw and a box of brightly coloured poster paints.

There was a very funny cartoon in the May issue of *The Oldie* which depicted modern tourists being thrown into hand-carts and a woman complaining: 'I had no idea the Plague was part of the mediaeval theme-restaurant experience.' This struck me as less amusing when we arrived at Riquewihr, a pretty-pretty Walt Disneyish mediaeval village crawling with Saturday punters. An oldie *Telegraph* hack and I decided to give the antique shops a miss and go for a beer, only to find ourselves sitting by an open sewer. Phew! Nobody ventured out to serve us. I suppose – sewer apart – we looked too much like journalists.

The one thing I am always looking for, no matter which part

of the world I'm in, is authenticity, whatever that is, but it is increasingly hard to find it. I caught just a whiff of it in the village of Kientzheim, where the hotel was of unbelievable austerity but where at least you got the feeling of ordinary Alsatians going about their daily business of producing dry Rieslings, spicy Gewürztraminers, aromatic Pinots and other white wines, and not just putting on a show for the tourists. (In Kientzheim, on a Sunday morning, I crept into the beautiful village church for a few moments of quiet – the only bit of peace on the press trip.)

By and large, Alsatian restaurants are a class up on their hotels. A typical dinner spread might be: celery soup, pâté de foie gras with salad, veal vol-au-vent with pasta, goat's cheese, sorbet with brandy, all accompanied, of course, by those rather pretentious Alsatian white wines... As a lover of vin rouge, I am at a disadvantage here, but I found the wines we were offered overrated and expensive.

After all this commercially based hospitality and the terrible strain of having to be nice to everybody all the time, it was a relief to be back in the pink cathedral city of Strasbourg and to sit down to a square meal of *tarte à l'onion* and *choucroute à l'ancienne*, two traditional regional specialities there is absolutely no beating. It was even more of a relief to get back to the good, honest peasant food of the *foyer*s: *crudités*, *blanquette de veau*, rice, and cream cheese were waiting for me at the end of the eight-hour journey back to Avignon, for which I was obliged to pay 200 francs in lieu of being thrown off the train at Colmar, the first time this has ever happened to me...

I feel a bit guilty about not sounding more enthusiastic about Alsace because Linda Hearn, the Inntravel boss, who accompanied us, is one of the nicest and most considerate businesswomen I have ever met and the concept of cheap, independent travel for older people is an admirable one. But I do not see how even thoughtful Linda could persuade two typical punters, a middle-aged couple from Solihull, say, that a walk through the hills and vineyards of Alsace constitutes a holiday experience not to be missed.

A New Orthodoxy

Turn right out of la gare d'Avignon, walk though *la gare routière* (the coach station) into the Avenue St Ruf, which you follow into the south-east suburbs of the city until it becomes Avenue du Moulin de Notre Dame. There is an ancient, ruined abbey to your left and a little park which you cross onto Avenue de la Reine Jeanne. Right in front of you, almost hidden among elm trees, is an exotic single-storey building. This is the Eastern Orthodox Church of St Cosmo and St Damian.

At the church entrance, shrouded in pink bougainvillea, oleander and bitter orange trees, a man in his late middle age, sporting a mauve shirt with matching bow tie, charming in a slightly sinister way, will greet you in impeccable French. He is the *concièrge non salarié* (unpaid janitor) of St Cosmo and St Damian. He is me, and has been for a couple of months...

There is a wonderful passage in Evelyn Waugh's *Brideshead Revisited* when Sebastian, the drunken protagonist, goes to work at a Roman Catholic monastery in North Africa. His devout younger sister, Cordelia, pointedly observes that there is always somebody around a monastery who is neither quite in it nor quite out of it: 'They had the idea of making him a sort of under-porter,' she says. 'There are usually a few old hangers-on in a religious house, you know, people who can't quite fit in either to the world or the monastic rule.' Sebastian goes on a binge now and again, disappears for a few days, but the monks always take him back. This – the booze apart – is pretty well my current situation.

How did it come about? The rather surprising answer is French TV, which I used to watch a good deal until I realised how bad it was compared with British TV. They have an ecumenical thing on a Sunday morning, *Le Jour de Seigneur*, covering all the faiths, and I couldn't help noticing that it was the bearded priests of the Eastern Orthodox Church who made by far the most sense: it is the obvious destination for anyone who is disenchanted with contemporary Catholicism but wishes to remain Catholic, as it were ('High' Anglicanism is a very inferior substitute).

When I got to Toulouse in 1996, I started going to the Russian Orthodox Church, which was in the same street as the Foyer Antipoul, where I was then living. Coincidence or *le Dieu* at work? I went along for several weeks, but I never spoke to anybody, just sat quietly at the back and soaked up the liturgy. The liturgy is long, make no mistake – three hours at least, four or five if there is a wedding or a baptism – but it is immensely rewarding, oddly moving and relaxing at the same time, if you are prepared to go along with it and listen intently as you would listen to, say, opera or classical music. Don't fight it. (I would recommend it to anyone who has been through a period of strain, as I have for some years now.)

Arriving in Avignon in 1997, I felt at a bit of a loss because it seemed unlikely that there would be an *église Orthodoxe* in such a small city. But determination and persistence (two vital qualities on the spiritual journey) paid off because I enquired at a religious bookshop in the city centre and they gave me the rather poetical address, 9 rue Poème du Rhône, which is where the Orthodox Church of St Cosmo and St Damian is situated.

It is not that easy to find (see first paragraph), but one freezing January morning I made my way there. There was a wedding taking place, which meant that the liturgy went on forever. Bernard, a 53-year-old hotel executive, was marrying a beautiful young Syrian girl, Waafa, which means fidelity. Bernard turned out to be a very jovial fellow with a British sense of humour and invited me to their reception for a glass or two of wine – badly needed after five hours of singing. We have remained friends ever since.

Things have just gone on from there. I have returned to St

Cosmo and St Damian each time I have been back in Avignon and found the Orthodox liturgy increasingly liberating. Although it doesn't seem like it at first, it is actually much less formal than the Roman Catholic Mass.

People come and go more or less as they please, wander round the church, light candles under the icons, chew on the holy bread, greet their friends … it is not unlike going to a party at the house of a very close acquaintance.

Bernard and Waafa, who has taken the French name of Anne and whom I have come to love, have been kind to me; they invited me to their country house in Provence. They introduced me to Dr Claude Hiffler, who is the lay secretary (or head) of the Orthodox Church for the whole of south-east France. And, of course, I have got to know the priest, Père Henri (a refugee from Catholicism), who combines the parish with being Professor of Economics at the University of Grenoble. Père Henri believes that the Roman Catholic Church is a dying institution. I have even met a Bishop, Monseigneur Paul, based in Nice, who turned out to be an Englishman, born in Suffolk, educated at Gordonstoun! 'Which public school did you attend?' he asked me kindly through his beard in which there would be room for several birds to nest. It did not seem to occur to him that I might not have gone to one.

I hope for 'Chrismation', that is, formal admittance to the Orthodox Church, some time next month. No doubt the liturgy will go on for ever that morning too. Becoming Orthodox is the end of a long spiritual journey for me – at least I hope it is the end (perhaps I shall embrace Judaism on my deathbed). Twenty years as an Anglican, 20 years agnostic, 20 years of Roman Catholicism. It is really like getting married for the third time. This time, I believe, it will last. The triumph of hope over experience?

It was the dynamic Dr Hiffler (another refugee from Catholicism) who suggested that I might take on the job of 'unpaid janitor' at their Avignon church, which means that I have also acquired superb free living accommodation (a nice change from the *foyers*) adjacent to the church which I have the use of all day, so I can say my own private prayers at 8 am and 6 pm, which I do faithfully. (Perhaps you will pray for me, if you ever pray.)

I am also turning out to be a good and efficient janitor. The thing I am best at is seeing off the many ecumenical groups who come along to St Cosmo and St Damian on weekday evenings (the Orthodox Church is surprisingly open to other faiths). The groups usually consist of highly respectable middle-class French people, the bourgeoisie, if you like, invariably the possessors of brand-new or almost-new posh motor cars. But St Cosmo and St Damian has no car park and is situated in the Arab quarter of Avignon. It is rather like living in a suburb of Algiers. (How do you know? Have you ever lived in Algiers? No, but I have read the novels of Albert Camus.) All I have to do is remind these naive people of what will happen to their beautiful cars if they leave them out too late. They then drive off amazingly quickly, leaving me to brood on my sins alone in the beautiful little church. Next morning, I wake up at about seven with a strange, unfamiliar feeling. It takes me some time to identify it. I think it is called happiness.

De'Ath Comes for the Archbishops

In 1970, a man named Michael De-la-Noy, press secretary to Michael Ramsey, Archbishop of Canterbury, arranged for me to interview the old boy for the *Illustrated London News*. I was unusually nervous, never having met anyone of such eminence, but the interview went extremely well. So well, in fact, that I felt able to telephone him a few weeks later and arrange a 30-minute interview for Radio 4. That went well, too, and Ramsey, who had by then sacked De-la-Noy for writing in 'gay' magazines, offered me the job of his press secretary.

I was reluctant to take this on (they were only offering £3,000 a year, not a great sum even in those days, and I had a non-working wife and two children to support) but agreed to hang around Lambeth Palace for a couple of months until he found someone else. This gave me a ringside seat at the heart of the Anglican Church which I have never forgotten.

Breakfast time at Lambeth was something to experience, with important business letters involving the appointment of Archdeacons etc ending up smeared with butter and marmalade (Ramsey hated administration) while the Ramseys scrabbled for their personal mail. (Having no children of their own, they were always looking – rather indiscriminately, I felt – for child substitutes. Once it had been De-la-Noy. For some time, it was me. Sooner or later, a fresh, pink-faced young curate would come along and they would transfer their affections to him. For me, that would be a relief.)

Ramsey's senior chaplain in those days was a dreadful man

named Geoffrey Tiarks, suffragan Bishop of Maidstone. When I say dreadful, what I really mean is that he was a dreadful snob. Ramsey and Tiarks detested each other and were not on speaking terms the entire time I was there. I would sometimes catch Tiarks listening outside the study door when I was closeted with Ramsey. Then he would ask me to lunch at some posh little restaurant in Westminster and grill me as to the Archbishop's thinking on some Church matter. 'You get on very well with him, don't you?' he said to me once, through gritted teeth.

The reason I got on so well with Michael Ramsey was that I liked to discuss theology with him and hated small talk as much as he did. One of my jobs was to arrange lunches for journalists from women's magazines who, overwhelmed by the surroundings, perhaps, would end up asking Ramsey about the roses in the Lambeth garden. Ramsey knew nothing about roses. But he knew a great deal about the theory of the Atonement. So, finally, he would rudely turn his back on the nice ladies and discuss theology with me.

Michael and Joan Ramsey were a simple, unsophisticated North Country couple who hated pomp and ceremony of any kind. I recall a very amusing moment when they lunched at 10 Downing Street while Edward Heath was Prime Minister, when oysters were served as the first course. Heath politely waited for the Ramseys to start eating but, of course, they didn't because they had never been offered oysters before and didn't know how to tackle them. So they waited for Heath to start... I thought we were going to sit there for ever.

In November 1974, when Ramsey resigned, I went along one afternoon to Lambeth to say good-bye and found him stretched out on a sofa, shoeless, one purple sock off, one still dangling, having just been to Buckingham Palace for a farewell lunch with the Queen. 'Who was there?' I asked. 'Oh, nobody much,' he murmured, 'Just the Queen and the corgis...'

In 1979, when I became a Roman Catholic, he wrote me a long, personal letter. He said he understood my reasons, that he envied me and felt inclined to follow but did not dare to, given his position. I now wish I'd kept that letter which was, in some ways, a historic document.

About this time, 1974, I went to see his successor, Donald Coggan, to talk about the press job again. (It was then being done by John Miles, an old BBC colleague.) Coggan was living in a poky flat in Victoria, having not yet moved into Lambeth. I knew at once that we should never get along. He struck me as a narrow man – full of evangelical platitudes. In fact, he brought back painfully and vividly my Lower Church evangelical background from which I am still, I guess, in flight.

Also, Coggan had a curious obsession with the Beatles. On learning that I had just been to New York to interview John Lennon, he kept asking what I had made of him: 'What was he like? A nice chap, I don't doubt,' he said over and over again. Well, there are many adjectives that might have been applied to Lennon but 'nice' was definitely not among them...

The Ramseys' departure from and the Coggans' move into Lambeth Palace was an acrimonious one. The two couples had never got along. Joan Ramsey refused to leave any of Michael's ornate, Anglo-Catholic investments behind: 'Mrs Coggan would probably have turned them into cushion covers,' she remarked.

In 1980, Alexander Chancellor, then editor of the *Spectator*, sent me to interview the new incumbent at Lambeth Palace, Robert Runcie, who has recently died. Runcie has been widely criticised for being too worldly, but I found him extremely spiritual. I have a good radar for spirituality and Runcie gave off the stuff in great gobs. At the same time, he seemed rather uncomfortable. I suspect that he didn't really want the job – or, rather, that, having wanted it, when he got it, he no longer wanted it. He told me that he felt the coming period of being Archbishop would contain some 'dark and dangerous times and much suffering'. He wasn't kidding.

Runcie's biggest – literally – problem was Terry Waite, whom he appointed as his adviser on Anglican communion affairs and whom he allowed far too much leeway at Lambeth, where Waite became a kind of cuckoo in the nest. There is a story, possibly apocryphal, of a woman journalist arriving at Lambeth and asking to see Waite and being told: 'I'm afraid Mr Waite's busy, but the Archbishop will see you, if you like.'

Years before he was taken hostage, I was commissioned by the *Times* to write a profile of Waite. While we were talking in his office, Runcie, in a filthy old raincoat and a scarf covering his dog-collar, stuck his head round the door and asked, 'Ready, Terry?' (The two used to sneak out for a drink at a little pub in Lambeth – they would sit in a corner and drink whisky and imagine, vainly, that nobody recognised them.) 'No, I'm not, I'm being interviewed by Wilfred De'Ath for the *Times*,' said Waite self-importantly. (When, years later, Waite was wheeling and dealing at the White House, he used to ring Runcie just to tell him where he was. 'I'm at the White House, Bob.' 'So what?' said Runcie.)

Back in 1982, Derek Jameson, then editor of the *News of the World*, offered me £500 to retell some anecdotes of the Runcie ménage. I am ashamed to say that I took his tainted gold, but I never told him my favourite, which concerned the evening Lindy Runcie, the lady wife, was entertaining some of her favoured students at a musical soirée at Lambeth. Runcie came in rather forlornly, having lost a button off his cassock just before he was due to go and preach. 'Would you mind sewing it on for me, dearest?' he asked her in his plaintive and rather sheep-like voice. She did so without a word, then threw the cassock on the floor at his feet while the students looked on. He bent humbly to pick it up. I suppose a little humility is good for an Archbishop.

Long-Lost Lust
in Lubéron

I am hoping for 'Chrismation', that is, formal admission to the Orthodox Church, early this month. When I went to see the parish priest to arrange this, I heard myself, by an odd slip of the tongue, asking for 'Cremation' instead. Père Henri looked a bit taken aback. 'I'm afraid that's really not possible,' he said dubiously. (In any case, I would have been using the wrong word, since the French for cremation is *incinération*. Sounds even worse, doesn't it?)

When we had got this linguistic difficulty out of the way, he gave me a piece of good advice: 'Why not take a short holiday before such a momentous step?' he suggested. So, being now the proud possessor of a pair of stout walking boots presented to me by Chris Brasher for my journey through the Vosges hills last May (*Oldie* 136), I decided to neglect my janitorial duties for a few days and set off into the Luberon *à la recherche du temps perdu*.

There was one unpleasant thing I had to do first, however, and that was to kill off my only companion in the Orthodox Church of St Cosmo and St Damian, a large brown rat. He had been disturbing me for some weeks and, being about the size of a small rabbit, was even able to knock over my substantial rubbish bin to get at the stale bread. But I still felt guilty when I asked Gébré, my well-meaning but hopelessly unreliable Ethiopian gardener, to bring along some rat poison. When Gébré finally remembered to do so, poor Rat was dead within a few hours. I found him stretched out under the oleander tree. It is a strange thing about living on one's own that normally anti-social animals, even inanimate objects, become like friends. I felt as though part of myself had died with Rat. Perhaps it had.

I set out for Lubéron. My first stop was Ménerbes, the village made famous by Peter Mayle in his books about Provence. Everyone at one time or another lived in Ménerbes, from the sublime (Picasso, Camus) to the ridiculous (Mayle). I lived there myself in the very early 1960s, trying to compile an anthology of English humour for French readers which was eventually published by Gallimard as *L'Humeur Anglais* and which can still be found in those little bookstalls along the Seine. My co-author and translator was Tony Mayer, then cultural attaché at the French embassy in London, who actually owned a large, beautiful, historic house, La Carnejane, in Ménerbes. Ménerbes in those pre-Mayle days was a totally deserted, remote mountain village and Tony and I lived there for months, working on our book, without electricity or running water and with only Tony's drunken Italian butler, Eugenio, for company.

I got off the coach at Les Baumettes, but I didn't linger because I still owe a four-star hotel there several thousand francs, dating back to 1994. I walked up the steep, three-kilometre climb towards Ménerbes and had just broken the back of it when a posh, elderly, English-speaking woman drew up and offered me a lift. She had a very slight French accent and I couldn't work out whether she was a very posh Frenchwoman or a very posh Englishwoman who had lived in France for so long that she had developed the accent. (It turned out to be the latter.)

I refused the lift rather abruptly since I was enjoying the walk, then immediately regretted doing so because it seemed to me that an excellent scrounging opportunity had gone amiss. However, I ran into her again in the village, as I hoped I would, and she turned out to be Madame Alicia de Brosses, no less, a widow once married to a Frenchman and currently the house guest in Ménerbes of Gimpel Fils (Jean Gimpel, author of *Les Bâtisseurs des Cathedrales* and brother Peter, purveyor of modern French art to the English bourgeoisie at their London gallery), who were Tony's old neighbours in Ménerbes and lived in an even posher house than he did (Tony died in 1997).

So, within a few minutes of arriving in Ménerbes, the Scrounger had fallen on his feet again. He was drinking iced beer by the Gimpel swimming-pool and being told by Catherine Gimpel, Jean's widow, that Ménerbes hadn't really been spoiled by Peter Mayle because the Japanese tour buses couldn't make it up the hill and through the tortuous village streets. Maybe not. But it looked pretty spoiled to me.

A wonderful lunch *chez* Gimpel followed – melon, marinated beef, haricots verts, goat's cheese, fresh cherries all washed down with a great deal of vin blanc and name-dropping reminiscences of many Provençal neighbours – Stephen Spender, Iris Murdoch, Dirk Bogarde – no longer with us.

Mid-afternoon, I set off to walk to Bonnieux (12 kilo-metres) in a nostalgic reverie, a drunken stupor and a drenching rainstorm. My dream was to stay at the same hotel, the Clerici, where I had lived with a very beautiful French-Swiss woman in the 1980s. The De'Ath luck held again because not only did the hotel have room but it gave me the same bedroom occupied by us two in the summer of 1985. There on the wall was the very dent made by Isabelle in a fit of jealous rage when she spotted me throwing a young, nubile, topless French girl into the hotel swimming-pool. 'You touched her breasts! I distinctly saw you touch her breasts!' As if I would do such a thing...

Well, if I did do such a thing, I was being punished for it now, 15 years later, because mine seemed to be the only room in the hotel not occupied by a young European couple making love. From above, from below, from either side, the orgasmic cries rang out, among which I could discern the German (guttural), the French (high-pitched), and the Italian (lyrical/operatic) among various other nationalities. I have to admit that this erotic Tour de Babel drove me to a pitch of sexual frustration such as I have never known.

Fortunately, it was a fine evening after the rain and there was one of those spectacular Lubéron sunsets – the most beautiful in Europe. I went out on to my balcony and tried to calm down. If you have never seen the sun set over the Lubéron mountains, then you should get a plane down to Avignon or Marseille right now and come and experience it (the autumn ones are especially beguiling).

I didn't hang around Bonnieux next morning because I owe money there as well, but *Oldie* readers will be pleased to learn that I did pay my hotel bill on this occasion – though I was tempted not to. I set off to walk the 12 kilometres to Apt through the vineyards (it looks like a good, rich crop this year). The art of walking through these hills – I managed 24 kilometres a day, 15 miles, but could do more – is to settle on a cruising speed (mine is 4 mph) and just keep going till you reach your destination. Don't be tempted to stop for a rest or even to slow down because you may find you can't get going again. A lesson for old age there?

In the flourishing little market town of Apt I took the risk of going to another hotel where I had never paid and ordered a coffee, then a beer. They were up to their old tricks of not bringing enough change or even not bringing it at all. When this had happened three times, I began to wonder if they had recognised me and were extracting their revenge. But the fact is the French just don't like giving you your change, let alone the right change. I could count on the fingers of one hand the times the change has been in my favour across these 40 years; whereas in that magic summer of 1985 in the Lubéron and elsewhere,

Isabelle and I were short-changed 37 times. I know this, because I kept count and wrote a pompous letter to the *Daily Telegraph* about it. It was the only fly in the ointment of our happiness – apart from the topless girl, of course.

Growth of a Beard

I wrote in *Oldie* 137 that becoming Orthodox was the end of a long spiritual journey for me. I was wrong, of course. What it is not is the end but another beginning. I realised this as soon as I had 'Chrismation' on 1 October. The ceremony itself was a bit of an anti-climax: I forgot most of my words and stumbled over the few I could remember. However, this only made the occasion more natural and sincere, according to the very supportive onlookers.

Père Henri, the parish priest, who presided, insisted that I remove my shoes and socks so he could anoint my bare feet with holy oil. I always welcome an opportunity to exhibit my naked feet in public since they happen to be my best physical feature, as a pretty Arab girl present was not slow to point out. I have even employed them as a seduction technique. I remember once… oh, but that was long ago and in another country and besides, the wench is dead.

Père Henri, who is not slow to give advice, also suggested that I make a short post-Chrismation retreat at the only Orthodox Monastery in Britain, at Tolleshunt Knights, near Maldon, in deepest Essex. So I was obliged to leave my beloved Avignon, still roasting in an Indian summer heatwave, for the cool, autumnal English countryside which I had not set foot in for 12 months. I will not describe the 36-hour train journey – it was, as the French say, *un cauchemar*, a nightmare! All the French trains ran to time, all the British ones were late. (I didn't pay on any of them.)

I arrived by bus at Tolleshunt Knights on a Tuesday lunchtime and, to my amazement, there seemed to be nuns everywhere:

Russian nuns, Greek nuns, Irish nuns, fat nuns, thin nuns, tall nuns, small nuns – about half turned out to be with a visiting group but, all the same, it was confusing, since Père Henri had assured me that I would find a monastery under the venerable Fr Kyrill and other bearded monks. As it turned out, there was scarcely a beard in sight. Even the Orthodox Church appeared to have gone unisex.

Lunch was a very strange meal, consisting of fried eggs with mashed potatoes. Anyone who knows about cooking will tell you that fried eggs cool down very quickly when exposed in a refectory. By the time the long and solemn Grace had been chanted and said, the eggs were hard, frozen, yellow bullets. But I was too hungry to mind very much. An 'Essex Girl' nun with a truly horrible voice did the accompanying reading from the Gospels. As I listened to her Estuary tones massacring the Holy Scripture, a profound depression settled on me. I asked myself – not for the first time in such circumstances – what on earth I was doing here when I could have been basking in sunny Provence. Perhaps I was just tired...

A siesta followed – I asked for a heater because my shabby room was damp and freezing – and then I took tea (an improvement on lunch) with the visiting (ecumenical) group. Supper, taken after two hours of chanting the Jesus Prayer – which consists of the words 'Lord Jesus Christ, Son of God, have mercy on us' endlessly repeated, mantra-fashion, in various tongues, Russian, Greek, French, etc – in the church, was another strange meal, some kind of very Slavonic fish with mixed vegetables. A disagreeable young nun who seemed to be growing a beard and a moustache (did she have ambitions to become a monk?) refused me a second cup of black tea because it was 'against the rules'. Afterwards, when I remonstrated, pleading post-travel dehydration, she changed tack and said it was because she had been too absorbed in the reading (being done by a fat French nun this time) to quench my thirst.

She didn't want to miss a word, she said. Well, I thought churlishly, you can't have it both ways…

After 24 hours or so, I realised that most of my initial dislike of the monastery sprang from travel fatigue and paranoia. Things began to look up when I encountered the elderly monks (they were much nicer than the young ones, who all sported aggressive black beards and angry scowls – would-be Rasputins to a man), of whom at least two were British. My mind began to settle down a bit. I was given a more cheerful room. It is like watching cloudy water disperse – suddenly you see the bright pebbles at the bottom of the lake. I began to enjoy myself.

I did everything wrong, of course. I sat on the wrong side – the nuns' side – in the highly decorated church; and the fat French nun hissed '*Etes-vous Orthodoxe?*' when she saw me crossing myself in the wrong way going up to Communion. But it didn't matter very much. That is the good thing about Orthodoxy – it is more relaxed than Catholicism. There is not the feeling that everyone is watching and sitting in judgment on you.

It was very hard to tell the older monks apart because they all wore their hair long – in pig-tails – and with those impressive beards for the birds to nest in. (The tradition began when shaving took 20 minutes – time better devoted to God in prayer, they thought. There is really no excuse for it now when you can shave in two minutes.) But I did finally discern Monk Silovan, the Guest-master, an ex-Winchester College member who is one of the only two Brits in the establishment.

Monk Silovan believes that Orthodoxy is creeping onto the map in Britain, as it has already done in France. He cites, perhaps a shade naively, the increasing use of the word 'icon', as in 'Princess Diana: Royal Icon', as well as the popularity of John Tavener's music, which is largely based on the Jesus Prayer and written with the help of an ancient Orthodox Abbess in Whitby. I think there may be more to it than that, but there is no disputing that the young nuns and monks here at Tolleshunt Knights are in an upbeat frame of mind. Perhaps, in embracing Orthodoxy, I may at last call myself a post-modernist: a member of a Western tradition, embracing ancient Eastern wisdom. Anyway, it feels like a new beginning and I am looking forward to it.

Lust and Loneliness

Sister Maria, a sexy little German nun, was assigned to drive me to the station at the end of my six-day retreat at the unisex Orthodox Monastery at Tolleshunt Knights in Essex. The Abbot, Fr Kyrill, bidding farewell, looked keenly at the pair of us, then murmured gravely 'I think you'd better take a chaperone'. So Sister Anastasia, the one growing a beard and a moustache and sporting NHS specs, was ordered to accompany us. Probably just as well. Enforced abstinence has left me so randy I could screw a snake. And Sister Maria's virginity, which I wouldn't have bet on, might have been in danger…

When you've just been 'Chrismated', as I have, and are, presumably, in a reasonable state of Grace, that's when the Devil really gets going. He fires every shot in his armoury at you. Apart from lust, there was the problem of gluttony: I found myself devouring huge quantities of the monastery's fish, fresh vegetables and fruit. In six days I put on nearly a stone, which I resolved to shed by walking to my next destination, Walsingham in north Norfolk, a distance of 60 miles. When the time came, though, I weakened and caught a train to Norwich.

I have written before about the vagaries of the Eastern Counties transport system. At the horrible Norwich bus station, the Walsingham bus was clearly posted to leave from Gate 4. (I confirmed this at the office.) When the time came, it left from Gate 8, leaving a number of indignant shoppers behind. The driver seemed unconcerned: 'They should know better,' he said shrugging. Nothing ever changes in this country.

In the holy village of Little Walsingham, England's Nazareth, in the Sue Ryder Retreat House, there was a beautiful Polish girl, Ola, working in the kitchen: 21 years old, blonde, blue-eyed, and with a figure to die for. At supper, she offered to accompany me the next morning on a walk to Great Walsingham in search of the Orthodox Church there. I could hardly believe my luck. I lay awake all night in my narrow cell throbbing with lust. The Devil was hard at work, no doubt about it.

When the right moment came and Ola was snuggling up against me in the deserted, darkened little church, I chickened out and gave her just a chaste kiss on her eyebrow. Well, she was my junior by 42 years and I am no Alan Clark. Saved by the bell! I resolved to knock sex on the head once and for all and live an entirely spiritual life from now on…

This wasn't easy. I thought a good start might be to walk to the nearby village of Sculthorpe (four miles), where an old friend, Ken Kightley, a former verger of St Giles, Oxford, lives a hermit-like existence in a little cottage. The cottage was cold and unprepossessing and there was something depressing about the hundreds of unread theological volumes (Ken had once planned to be ordained) mildewing in the damp Norfolk air. If this was sainthood, then it wasn't for me.

What is sainthood anyway? It is the desire – and the attempt – to live a perfect life. It has its dangers because when it all comes crashing down, as it almost inevitably must, you may go from one extreme to the other and end up in prison, as I have done more than once. Perhaps it is better and wiser to steer a middle course.

Talking of steering, I next went in search of another old friend and Oxford contemporary, Fr Philip Steer, who was ordained into the Anglican Church but is now an Orthodox priest somewhere in these parts. To discover his whereabouts, I went along to Great Walsingham for Saturday Vespers, but there were only five people present, including myself: a tiny spinster church mouse, an elderly couple and a single pilgrim. And this is said to be one of the most flourishing Orthodox parishes in Britain! God knows what the others must be like!

At the Sunday liturgy next morning, there were even fewer of us (the pilgrim had gone on his way). The married couple, Richard and Pauline, who were very nice, told me that Fr Steer, having given up the parish for reasons that were by no means clear, now lived in a remote village, Binham, three miles beyond Great Walsingham. The following Wednesday, I set out to walk over there in the mid-autumn rain. He seemed pleased to see me.

At Oxford, in the late 1950s, Philip Steer was a name to conjure with in university theatre. (He directed Jonathan Cecil and myself in *Char*, John Spurling's first play, an overnight sensation at the Oxford Playhouse in 1959.) I must say I always thought he would enter that profession. But he chose ordination and the spiritual path.

Now he lives in deep, bearded seclusion in a run-down cottage, supported by his second wife, Philippa, a nurse. He has his own tiny Orthodox chapel in a shed in the back garden where he says the Liturgy for himself and his family. To live in such a remote location is, as he suggested to me over tea, in itself a form of extremism, like taking hard drugs or living on a macro diet. As his former parishioner Richard said to me, 'Father Philip may be too spiritual for his own good.' It had not occurred to me before that it might be possible to be too spiritual. That can be as dangerous as being too worldly. In contrast with his deep, indubitably sincere spirituality, Fr Philip soon began to make me feel extremely worldly again. But I think I prefer it that way.

Just Call Me Fred

I am beginning to understand the relief felt by Lawrence of Arabia when he called himself Aircraftsman Shaw; or by Oscar Wilde when, after his imprisonment, he called himself Sebastian Melmoth. In Britain, I am still the raffish international criminal and journalist, Wilfred De'Ath. Here in France they call me 'Fred of the Foyers' or, even more simply, 'Foyer Fred'. (The French can't get their tongues round my first name, but 'Fred' is the perfect sobriquet for an Englishman down on his luck.)

I cut short my autumn journey through England after a nightmare train journey from Norwich to Brighton which took 18 hours instead of the scheduled six. The last stage of the journey, from London to Brighton, which should have taken an hour, took four-and-a-half. We were re-routed and made to change trains at Gatwick Airport, Three Bridges and Littlehampton, and eventually reached Brighton at 2 am, so I was obliged – not for the first time in my chequered progress – to spend the night on the streets. Next day, I took another very slow, stopping train to Portsmouth harbour, swearing never to set foot in this beleaguered. God-forsaken, paralysed country again. (I know I have said this before, but this time I mean it.) What with the floods, the non-functioning railways and Mad Cow Disease, life in France seems a picnic in comparison, although as I write the French are getting their first taste of the last-named – the pot has called the kettle black just once too often.

116

So I plunged back into the *foyers* and tried to make life a bit easier for myself by learning to go with the flow. This is something I have been trying to teach myself ever since National Service days in the 1950s when, having just deliberately failed to get a commission in an infantry regiment, I was billeted with two other BAOR squaddies, Tony and Norman, serial adulterers both. That made three of us, though my taste leaned more in the direction of blowsy, slightly over-ripe German women than to the syphilitic Naafi girls of their preference. It was only when I brought myself down to their level and realised that I was really no better than they were that Tony, Norman and I became best friends for life.

It was a lesson I had to learn all over again when I was sent to prison in 1993 for sundry hotel offences. The temptation when you are sent to prison for the first time is to pretend it is not happening, to pull the covers over your head, miss out on your morning cornflakes and wish the rest of the world was far away. This, I tell you from bitter experience, is an absolutely fatal policy. I owe a great deal to Dave, my first cell-mate, a hopeless alcoholic from Manchester, who pointed out that I wasn't handling prison well because I was refusing to 'go with the flow'. He was right. I took his words to heart, got off my bunk and started to take an interest in my fellow inmates. I even began to help a young armed robber with his plea in mitigation. It wasn't a very successful plea in mitigation. A first offender, Glenn had been 'looking at' probation until he met me. He ended up doing seven-and-a-half years. Well, that's the luck of the draw. Or, rather, that's the luck of which side of the bed the judge got out of…

I tried to bear this hard-learned lesson in mind when I was sent to prison again in 1998. This time, I practised with the officers who are, as a generalisation, even more degraded than the men they are paid to look after. A middle-aged prison officer named John Ridd entered my cabin (on the prison ship) and I at once pointed out that he rejoiced in the name of the protagonist of RD Blackmore's West Country novel, *Lorna Doone*. He nearly collapsed in astonishment. 'That's the first time in 20 years as a screw that an inmate has noticed that,' he said. Encouraged by this tribute to my literary knowledge, I began to help another young officer who was doing an Open University course in English Lit. This was so successful that he invited me to tea with himself and his wife (against the rules in any case) after my release, but I drew the line at that…

Now, in the French *foyers*, I am faced with the problem of how to go with the flow all over again. The other night, at the disgusting *foyer* in Caen, being very tired, I was filthily rude to an elderly Scotsman. I told him I hated his dog (which I did) and I cut him up quite badly in the canteen queue at supper. Next morning, feeling better and penitent, I apologised handsomely and profusely for my discourtesy. He accepted the apology with equal magnanimity and now we are bosom pals.

In Saumur, at the Foyer de 4 Saisons, I sit next to Serge, who is interested in amateur dramatics. I listen patiently to his tales of play selection, casting, rehearsals, technical problems, etc. In fact, I think I am the best audience he has ever had. Mind you, there is an element of cupboard love here because Serge is also the *foyer* cook, and the largest portions and choicest morsels are invariably mine in return for an attentive ear. At the same table sits Gilbert, an old man dying of emphysema. It was he who first christened me 'Foyer Fred' and the name has stuck.

Here in Limoges, in a sudden fit of generosity, I presented young Eric, who is *au chômage* (out of work), with my second-best watch. Now he follows me around like a little dog and can't do enough for me. It is almost embarrassing to discover how easily a Frenchman's affection is won. In Avignon, I have turned Patrick, *le sous directeur* of Visa *foyer*, who both speaks and understands English and who is, rather improbably, a graduate of the Sorbonne, into an *Oldie* reader. He can hardly wait for each month's new issue to arrive. Now that is really going with the flow.

Paperback Wastrel

Just when you think you can't sink any lower, then you do. At present, my monthly pittance not having arrived, I'm reduced to begging for my bread on the *merde de chien*-encrusted French streets. I fell into this, as I have fallen into so many things in France, indeed into so many things in my strange life, by chance. I was standing outside a church in Limoges in the rain (no big deal because it always rains in Limoges), minding my business, my hat in my hand – a rather natty little fedora, if you must know – when someone put 36 francs (about £3.60) into it. Enough for four lunches at La Bonne Assiette, Limoges' *restaurant social*. Since then, I haven't looked back.

Here in Avignon, a rich town, it seems even easier, although I've learned from bitter experience that it is the poor, not the rich, who give. You stand outside the snooty little Cathedral after Sunday Mass, hat in hand, and score about 50 francs (£5) in as many minutes, enough for ten lunches at Visa *foyer*'s excellent restaurant. I always thought I'd be too ashamed and embarrassed to beg, but it seems that I'm not. Hunger, as Charlie Chaplin said, has no conscience. The French public are generous and take it for granted, especially at Christmas, that they must give to the poor. On Christmas Eve, I took 63 francs and a single luncheon voucher. Nothing daunted, I returned to the fray on Christmas Day and cleaned up 450 francs (£45) in four hours. I went into a very chic hotel, the Palais des Papes, to turn all the change into notes and the girl cashier, who recognised me, since I've often stayed there, looked a bit surprised: 'Anyone would think you'd been begging on the streets,' she said.

It is not quite so easy at my own church, the Orthodox Church of St Cosimo and St Damian, because having once been their *concièrge non salarié* (unpaid janitor) I know almost everybody there and it really is a shade embarrassing to have to ask them for money. So I've taken to stealing the candle money instead. The Orthodox Church lights candles exclusively for the dead, and since I don't really believe in a life after death (I've never understood why belief in God predicates belief in an after-life) it seems sensible to me to use the money that would otherwise just go up in smoke to keep my ageing carcass on the road. I doubt whether Père Henri, our somewhat authoritarian parish priest, would agree. (Last Sunday I took 100 francs, enough for 20 Visa lunches.)

The fact is, morale is very low just at present. It must be, because I found myself taking a Jeffrey Archer novel (*The Fourth Estate*) out of the library's English section – invariably, along with Frederick Forsyth, a sign of severe demoralisation with me. I put it back pretty quickly, however, and retreated to Shakespeare, Avignon's English bookshop. Shakespeare is the best English bookshop in France. I will go further. It is the best English bookshop in Europe, and that includes England. It has all the books I have ever wanted to own – and some.

To begin with, it doesn't seem very promising. It always looks shut and the owner, a 79-year-old German Jew named Wolfgang Zuckermann, is not particularly friendly. This must be a kind of sales pitch in reverse because I found myself buying up Evelyn Waugh's *Brideshead Revisited*, E M Forster's *Howards End* and a life of F Scott Fitzgerald in order to impress him with my literary taste. It seemed to work because he suddenly became more approachable. Now I go in there every Saturday morning to drink coffee (he has a pleasant *salon de thé* at the back), read the

International Herald Tribune, listen to Haydn and Mozart on France Classique, and generally bask in the sweet, decaying aroma of good second-hand books, mostly paperbacks. I chew the fat with Wolfgang, who hates the modern world, cars, TV, the Internet, cell-phones, personal stereos, piped music, shopping malls, baseball caps whether worn straight or reversed, almost as much as I do. Wolfgang is an atheist, otherwise he would probably agree with the American priest I met recently at the Orthodox Monastery in Tolleshunt Knights in Essex that all these things, but most especially anything to do with computers, are actually the work of the Devil. As one who has not even properly graduated from the pen to the typewriter, let alone the word-processor, I find myself in total agreement.

The one thing Wolfgang does not dislike, apart from books, is young girls. Or perhaps I should say young women. (I haven't been able to bring myself to tell him that he is known as the Humbert Humbert of Avignon – an explicit reference to Nabokov's *Lolita*, one of our favourite books of all time.) No pretty girl, whether English, French, German or American, enters his shop without being deftly summed and chatted up. To put it bluntly, it is a girl trap. The stupid ones, however attractive, are either rejected out of hand or passed on to his friends, so this Christmas I have had my hands full with Sandrine, Marie, Deborah. Stephanie, Anna, Louise, Agnes and goodness knows who else. Wolfgang sets his standards so high that even the stupid ones are, by my reckoning, extremely bright.

Shakespeare, to sum up, is a little oasis of genuine civilisation away from the horror of the streets and from the rather artificially cultural atmosphere of Avignon itself, which is, basically, a small Provençal market town posing as the cultural centre of the universe. As a bookshop, even if it is not precisely 'where charming old gentlemen browse eternally among calf-bound folios', it is not far removed from it. It is impressive evidence, to quote Orwell again, of books as 'a humane trade which is not capable of being vulgarised beyond a certain point'. Anyway, it has been my salvation through the past lean month and I'm extremely grateful to it.

King of the Road

I have received a number of letters from *Oldie* readers asking me why I have chosen to live as I do. This month's article, based on actual experience, is by way of explanation…

Assuming, being penniless, I could raise the readies to cross the Channel and, being homeless as well, find accommodation in a night shelter in an English provincial city – Winchester, say, or Salisbury or Exeter – and, being still penniless, raise the £2 or £3 per night or whatever these places charge, I would still not be a happy man. My fellow residents would consist, almost exclusively, of stinking, alcoholic tramps; what little of their mottled skin appeared between their filthy whiskers would be covered in bruises and livid, open cuts sustained in recent street brawls. The police would be called to the shelter almost every night to sort out knife fights, etc.

Despairing of such pathetic scum, I would try to form friendships with the night shelter staff. They, however, would be understandably suspicious of a well turned-out, spick-and-span 'gentleman tramp' who still trims his beard twice a day and cleans his teeth after every meal. They would assume, not entirely wrongly, that an international fraudster had arrived to share their humble, provincial existence.

On the first suitable weekday, I would crawl along to the local DHSS office to sign on as unemployed. After a long delay, usually about three weeks, twice the estimated time, a very small giro cheque, about £50, would be issued. This, however, would be sent to an old address, since the DHSS computers are invariably one address behind, and would be lost. After a further painful delay, another minuscule cheque would be issued to the night shelter address, but that would be stolen either by a resident or, as happened to me more than once, by one of the staff, leaving me still penniless.

By now about five weeks would have passed. Despairing of ever receiving any money, and hunger having no conscience, as I said last month, I would have resorted to shoplifting once again. I am not a particularly skilful shoplifter and, sooner or later, I would be arrested and, given my previous record and the fact that I am, in any case, in breach of a Probation Order in East Sussex dating back to 1999, I would be sent to prison for a long time. (Some people, I know, say that prison is the best place for me, but it does not solve my problems and it costs the state upwards of £500 a week.)

About 20 years ago, when I was first divorced and sleeping rough and eating out of discarded Kentucky Fried Chicken cartons, I wrote an article for the *Guardian* about what I called the 'existential advantages' of such a life. These are infinitely compounded here in France, even in the disgusting Cap Horn Foyer in Caen where I am currently living and where your every movement, including that of your bowels, is kept under close observation – and commented on – by both staff and residents.

The actual advantages include: complete freedom to do as I please between the hours of 7 am when the *foyer* closes and 7 pm when it reopens; the use of the superb Caen public library, when it manages to open; the intellectual companionship, not of tramps, but of ordinary middle- and working-class Frenchmen temporarily down on their luck; and really excellent food.

Speaking of food, amusing things keep happening. Each weekday, I either walk or jump the bus to a distant suburb of Caen where some kind Roman Catholic ladies provide a free lunch, of which there is supposed to be no such thing. My fellow lunchers are all French tramps. The other day, someone had the macabre notion of crowning us all with golden cardboard crowns left over from Christmas. So I sat and ate my steak *haché* and rice in the company of 13 grisly kings of the road. When I went to wash my hands, I noticed my own crown atop my natty little fedora and I couldn't help thinking that I looked pretty distinguished… No wonder the proud, republican French, who in fact deeply envy us our monarchy, were bowing ironically low to *sa gracieuse Majesté*, as they called me. Well, they shouldn't have beheaded their own King…

Bog Standard

It was F Nietzsche who wrote that anything that doesn't actually kill you will make you stronger. This consoling observation returned to me after a month at Cap Horn, the disgusting *foyer* at Caen. To find it, you walk down an extremely depressing street, the rue de Marais, alongside the railway track. At the end is a large iron gate, crowned with barbed wire, where you are interrogated by a brutal-looking man in a leather jacket: 'Do you drink?' 'No.' 'Do you smoke?' 'No.' 'Do you sleep with young women?' 'No. *Et avec des vieilles non plus*,' I added humorously. He didn't crack a smile.

The resemblance to a concentration camp is overwhelming. Barbed wire apart, there is an observation tower, even sniffer dogs. Having, I guess, an overdeveloped sense of humour, which has seen me through many such situations, I couldn't resist asking: '*Où sont les chambres de gaz*?' That didn't make him smile either.

A horrible supper is served: tongue of beef with purée (mashed potatoes). The tongue is obviously off. Ten of us spend the night between the bathroom sinks to vomit and the filthy latrines to do the other. At one point, I find myself literally racing between the two. We are food-poisoned thus twice within five days.

My two room-mates, both ageing alcoholics, clearly hate the English. If the remarks they address to me and exchange between themselves (which they think I don't understand) through the long nights were addressed to Africans, Chinese or Arabs, they would find themselves being prosecuted for racism. But England remains the ancient enemy of France – and there is some residual resentment for the wartime bombing of Caen, which the French considered unnecessary – so anything goes.

Life at Cap Horn is so totally ghastly that I began to suspect myself of masochism for even wanting to stay there. But it is convenient – and cheap: 11 francs a night, and you don't even have to pay that if you haven't got it. But it is still a high price to pay for being abused by the prematurely senile, chain-smoking French tramps who sit just outside the latrines all through the night and give a running commentary on your bowel movements...

Partly to escape from these horrors – will my *via dolorosa* never end? – and partly to assuage a severe bout of homesickness, I started going to Dolly's, Caen's English teashop, just beside the castle. It has blue check tablecloths and is exactly the kind of place you would find in an upmarket English provincial city – Bath, say, or Cheltenham or Leamington Spa. In their shop, Dolly's sells Branston pickle and Cheddar cheese and Heinz baked beans and other products calculated to make you feel even more homesick. The French love it, since it saves them the trouble of crossing the Channel to experience their idea of *la vie anglaise.*

Dolly's is presided over by a rather fussy ex-cop from Kent (Steve), his charming wife (Dolly) and their sexy daughter, Elise, who speaks wonderful French. I spent so much time in there drinking cup after cup of real English Typhoo tea and eyeing up Elise, who is young enough to be my granddaughter, that I began to deceive myself into thinking that dear old Blighty was the place after all and that I ought to return there at once and try to put my chaotic life in order.

A few days at a horrible guest house in Southsea was more than enough to disabuse me of any such notion. I paid £25 a night to have a sulky, unshaven youth, a failed professional footballer, serve me with an inadequate and overcooked breakfast – bacon burnt to a crisp and eggs like golf balls. His language had to be heard to be believed. Conscientiously paying my way for once (what is happening to me? Am I going straight at last?), I was obliged to creep out into the Portsmouth drizzle each morning to buy a

Murdoch newspaper I didn't want in order to provide him with the change he didn't have.

Soon I began to miss the very privations of dear old Cap Horn, the hostel from hell, notorious throughout metropolitan France. After all, it didn't kill me, as at one point I thought it might, and I have now returned to the soothing, sunlit warmth of Avignon where, in the midst of winter, you can feel the inventions of spring. This is not my line but Lawrence Durrell's (*Justine*), and it expresses just what I now feel – hope and confidence in a brighter future.

Food for Thought

I am sorry (and a little ashamed) to report that, after only six months, I am becoming disillusioned with the Orthodox Church. I forget the correct word for paying more attention to the outward forms and elaborate ceremonials of religion (ritualism?) instead of to what is, or should be, at the heart of religion, i.e. God, but whatever it is the Orthodox Church, in France at least, is suffering from a very bad case of it.

Things came to a head for me on the third Sunday of Lent when the Greek Monseigneur Jérémie, Metropolitan Archbishop of Paris in the Patriarchate of Constantinople, came down to consecrate our little church of St Cosmo and St Damian. (It has taken him 19 years to get round to it: the church was actually built in 1982.) He arrived in state at Avignon station on the Saturday afternoon, accompanied by various black-bearded acolytes (more Rasputin clones) and a number of thuggish bodyguards, the leader of whom bore a disconcerting resemblance to the late Greek toad, Aristotle Onassis.

To see our elderly parish priest, Père Henri, and our Church President, the excellent Dr Claude Hiffler, grovelling in front of the assembled prelates on the station platform when they emerged from their private first-class apartment was stomach-churning stuff. To hear that they were then to be wined and dined, at our little church's expense, at the most chic restaurant in the city made me feel even worse…

Next morning, the ceremonies got under way at 8 am and continued through until 2 pm. They came to a grinding halt quite early when one of the accompanying acolytes spotted an elderly parishioner at the back sitting down. They could not proceed, he indicated brusquely, until he had got up from his chair, like everyone else. So I had to stand up. (Beneath a thin veneer of liberalism, the Orthodox Church is extremely authoritarian, and I'm afraid it brings out the rebel in me. I refuse to join a bunch of garlic-breathed, superstitious Greeks jumping to their feet like synchronised flick knives every time a bearded staretz flicks his fingers.)

We then proceeded reasonably smoothly until it was time for everybody to move into the church garden, carefully tended last summer by yours truly, for the actual rite of consecration. I took advantage of the church being empty to steal 20 francs (£2) from the candle money. Unfortunately, I was spotted by the Onassis lookalike standing in the church doorway, who immediately grassed me up to Dr Hiffler, who acted pretty reasonably in the circumstances, merely asking me to replace the money and leave the party forthwith.

This I was only too glad to do, since it meant that I was spared the sight of Monseigneur Jérémie and Monseigneur Raymond, the infinitely cunning Roman Catholic Archbishop of Avignon, hugging and kissing each other in a triumphalist and (to my mind) totally false display of ecumenical co-operation. Pass the sick-bag, Alice. (The chances of these two ever actually working together to further the kingdom of God are roughly equal to mine of becoming a Hassidic Jew.)

After these apparently endless rituals (six hours) the two Archbishops and their teams were treated to yet another slap-up-meal, with accompanying wines, at our expense. I did not actually get to see the menu because I was excluded from it but, judging by the groaning tables in the church refectory, it was not unlike the meal described by Elizabeth David in *French Provincial Cooking* which was consumed by a honeymoon couple on a river steamer in Rouen in 1855: 'Soup, fried mackerel, beefsteak, French beans, fried potatoes, an omelette *fines herbes*, a *fricandeau* of veal with sorrel, a roast chicken garnished with mushrooms, a hock of pork served upon spinach, an apricot tart, three custards, an endive salad, a small roast leg of lamb with chopped onion and nutmeg sprinkled upon it, coffee, two glasses of absinthe, *eau dorée*, a Mignon cheese, pears, plums, grapes and cakes. With the meal: two bottles of Burgundy and one of Chablis.'

I enjoy my food (and drink) as much as the next man but, 146 years later, watching these already overweight prelates stuffing and guzzling, the penny finally dropped. What the French actually worship is not God but good food. Food, in fact, is their true religion. The entire day revolves around it. How many times have I, dining *en famille*, heard a husband ask his wife, as he chomps on his lunchtime cassoulet: '*Délicieux, chérie, mais qu'est ce qu'on mange ce soir?*' ('Delicious, darling, but what are we having for dinner?') How relieved he is to learn that a fine *choucroute* awaits him that evening! God is, indeed, good to the French.

Just Desserts?

A rriving at Portsmouth harbour very early in the morning for the Oldie of the Year lunch, I did something I have never done before. I jumped a National Express coach to London. The trick is to tell the clerk that you will pay the driver and the driver that you have paid the clerk. If you choose the moment when the former is stowing luggage aboard, he doesn't look to see whether you have a ticket. It's a simple as that.

Successful theft is exhilarating. Invigorated by the saving of £12 and by the sight of the green, disease-ridden English countryside and the pretty, relatively unwrecked Hampshire villages, not glimpsed for many years, I was further cheered at the lunch by the chairman, Terry Wogan, telling me that I am the best thing in *The Oldie*. I expect he says this to all the contributors, but it was sweet music to my ears nonetheless. Intoxicated by free champagne and by the Great Tel's praise, not even my table companion, Zenga Longmore, telling me that I was actually the worst could dampen my high spirits. That's show business.

It was only a flying visit – I was jumping the train down to Portsmouth again by 4 pm (I got caught this time, but what the hell), and being swindled by Brittany Ferries, who seem to make up the prices as they go along, for the night crossing, which is hard to jump – but sufficient to convince me that dear old Blighty was the place after all, so I set out on a serious campaign to leave France after the best part of a decade, and settle in England again.

How to begin when you have no money and no prospect of any? First off, I wrote to Lord (Melvyn) Bragg, an old friend from Oxford and BBC days, who was meant to be at the lunch, sitting opposite me, but, in the end couldn't make it. Melvyn has been a loyal pal over many years and always good for a crisp £20 or even £50 when the going gets really rough. Then I telephoned my son Charles in Liverpool and asked him to send me enough money for the Channel crossing…

In the midst of these preparations, I came upon an interesting article in the *New Yorker* about the novelist Paul Bowles, who wrote *The Sheltering Sky*. Bowles was an expatriate homosexual American who died recently in Tangier at the age of 88. *The Sheltering Sky* – you may remember the rather bad film – is a bleak account of human beings confronting their ultimate destinies in the North African desert. It has been described as a vision not of an alternative life but of an escape from life altogether. Bowles himself observed, 'The shade is insufficient, the glare is always brighter as the journey continues. And the journey must continue – there is no oasis in which one can remain.' He was also fond of quoting Kafka's aphorism: 'From a certain point onward there is no longer any turning back. That is the point that must be reached.'

These words stuck me like a thunderbolt. Was I not, in planning to return to the green and pleasant land, guilty of merely 'turning back'? It was as if Melvyn were to give up *The South Bank Show* to edit the *Cumbria Gazette*, or Ingrams to resign from *The Oldie* to edit a newspaper for young people. Instead of dreaming of passing my declining years in some 'idyllic' village in Dorset, say, or Hampshire or Norfolk, should I not be plunging, as summer ripens, into the pitiless heat and light of southern France, of Spain, even north Africa?

After some internal debate, instead of retiring to England, that is what I have decided to do. First step: Tarbes in the Pyrenees, then Spain, then Morocco, perhaps even Algeria and the Sahara desert. For some years now, I have come to regard myself, since no one else has been prepared to do so, as my own existential hero, in love with my own myth, if you like, and prepared to go wherever the furtherance of that myth may lead me. It will be, to quote D H Lawrence, a savage pilgrimage, for sure. But it should provide good *Oldie* reading.

Brushes with De'Ath

On the night of 21 April, a large part of the ramparts of Saumur Castle fell into the Loire, slicing through the Foyer des 4 Saisons like a doll's house. Two of my friends in the room next door were badly injured. Fortunately, it was the weekend, so our little *foyer* was almost empty, otherwise there would have been more casualties, even fatalities. (Interviewed on television, the Mayor of Saumur was asked if there had been a recent inspection of the ramparts: 'Well, not recent, no.' 'When exactly?' 'Some time in the 16th century.')

This was my sixth brush with death in France in ten years. In the early nineties, the whole of the ancient city centre of Rennes, the capital of Brittany, caught fire. Luckily, my hotel was just on the perimeter. A few years later, I was 'jumping' the Grand Hotel de l'Opéra in Toulouse when the building was set alight from basement to roof. I was ignominiously rescued by firemen who, presumably, didn't care whether or not I was a fare-paying passenger. It was one way of coping with the problem of the bill, at any rate. In 1998, precisely the same thing happened to me at the station hotel in Caen in Normandy.

Later that year, an extremely violent ex-legionnaire went berserk in the *foyer* in Tarbes in the Pyrenees (where I'm writing this) during a row over the washing-up and let off several rounds from a heavy-duty pistol he shouldn't have been carrying. I felt a bullet whistle past my stomach, so I dived to the ground. Quite recently, in Limoges, somebody launched a fully laden rubbish bin at me from a fourth-floor window. It missed by inches. A passer-by thought it was a deliberate assassination attempt. I took the view that the Grim Reaper, frustrated by so many failed attempts on my life, was having a last shot…

A perceptive friend once observed that I am a person to whom things happen. All these close shaves have, naturally, concentrated my mind wonderfully on the subject of my own mortality. I have come to the rather obvious conclusion that death is not something that can be experienced from the outside. Travel firms delight in producing glossy brochures depicting the exteriors of beautiful trains and boats and planes, but when you actually travel in one you never get to see the outside of the vehicle. You only experience the journey from the inside. Death is like that.

We experience the death of our friends in this way, at second hand. The sad demise of colleagues and contemporaries like Peter Cook, Willie Rushton, Dennis Potter, Jeffrey Bernard, John Wells, Jennifer Paterson, Auberon Waugh, has left me numb but dry-eyed because, after all, these people led enormously successful and fulfilled lives and went down, as it were, with all their guns blazing. The death of two other friends, Tricia Haynes and Ian Lyon, filled me with a paroxysm of grief when they died because they had both led unfulfilled lives. You will have heard of neither of them, for that reason. (Tricia Haynes wrote extremely sensitive novels but never persuaded anyone to publish them. She died of cancer in her early fifties. Ian Lyon was a brilliant ex-president of the Oxford Union, one of the wittiest men I have ever known, but he somehow never made anything of his media career, although he did, briefly and unsuccessfully, edit the *Illustrated London News*. He died from AIDS in the early nineties.)

Where do I fit into this pantheon? Not with the first group, obviously, but not really with the second either. Not having had very much else to do for the past 20 years, I venture to suggest that I have brooded more intensely on the subject of death than anyone else I know. Having finally decided that there is nothing afterwards, or nothing that we can discern at any rate, I have resolved to enjoy whatever number of years are left to me. Paul Bowles in *The Sheltering Sky* makes the interesting observation that not knowing the date of our own demise adds a totally false sense of infinitude to our lives here on earth. If we knew precisely when we were going to die, our lives would suddenly seem extremely finite. We would have to recognise that we would only be able to do the things we enjoy again for a limited number of times. I, for instance, would have to accept that I am only going to make a few more exciting journeys through Europe; eat only another handful (mouthful?) of delicious French meals; screw only a few more sexy young girls...

The late Mark Boxer – sorry about all this posthumous name-dropping – once told me that he believed that people had some kind of mystic connection with their surnames, became like them in some curious kind of way. This was certainly true in his case – beneath an urbane exterior, Mark was very aggressive and competitive – and I suppose that it is true in mine too. All my life I have thought about death. I think about it even more these days. I think about it even more than I think about sex, which is saying something.

Dan Proposes,
but God Disposes

An Intelligent Person's Guide to Atheism
BY DANIEL HARBOUR

D aniel Harbour, who looks about 14 in his smirking jacket photo, says that his book is intended to be read in a 'comfortable afternoon beside a swimming-pool'. Having unaccountably mislaid my swimming-pool, I decided to substitute a bench beside the lake in the beautiful Jardin Massey in Tarbes, where I am currently living. The arrival of his pleas for atheism coincided with my own increasing conviction that man has invented God because he finds the thought of being alone in the universe intolerable. (This leaves me in the position of Larry, Somerset Maugham's protagonist in *The Razor's Edge*, a deeply religious man who cannot bring himself to believe in God.) So I was pleased to receive some (apparent) confirmation of my recent thinking.

I suppose I am as intelligent as the next person, but you would need to be some kind of intellectual genius to get through these 140 densely packed pages in the course of an afternoon, pool or no pool. Who said that a worthwhile book should be as hard to read as to write? I quote a random sentence from Chapter One: 'The meritocratic nature of rational enquiry extends even to its Spartan starting assumptions, which are essentially methodological.' Hmm. I think I'm going to have to take this rather slowly...

Harbour's big central idea is that what he pretentiously labels 'the Spartan meritocracy', i.e. atheism, has done more for the world than 'the Baroque monarchy', i.e. theism, and should therefore be adhered to. This thesis, which I find unconvincing, is developed in a weird, often scintillating, sometimes slipshod mid-Atlantic prose: 'By considering a wide range of evidence, historical and ethical, aesthetic and personal, I show that the logical superiority of atheism over theism, or of one world view over its opposite, is replicated at the practical level. So, this provides a second argument for the preferableness of atheism.'

The young philosopher's arrogance is breathtaking. Descartes ('that French guy who was wrong a lot'), Kant and several other world-famous thinkers are consigned to the dustbin of history, so that one is left with the impression that only what Daniel Harbour, ex-Balliol, currently Massachusetts Institute of Technology, believes can possibly be true. (He may be an 'intellectual steamroller', as the jacket claims, but he wears his erudition heavily and can't resist showing it off on every page. There is also too much special pleading, for my taste, on behalf of Jews and homosexuals.)

He does make one or two telling points. 'When technology is employed for evil, that evil is a reflection of the implementer, not of the technology they [sic] abuse.' Well said. 'A truly Christian society would have to be one where no one were [sic] ever punished, where no one owned or owed anything, and which would give any portion of its wealth to any individual or organisation that asked for it.' Well said again, Daniel, but when will you learn some grammar?

It was dear old Oldie of the Year John Mortimer who once remarked that it takes as much faith to be an atheist as it does to be a believer. Strangely enough, the effect this little book had on me was to enable me to believe in God, ontologically at least, all over again. I was, truth to tell, in very low water when I read it. No money for new clothes. No money for anything. No money full stop. Sitting by the lake, I prayed very hard to the God Daniel Harhour doesn't want us to believe in and, lo and behold, a man left his wallet behind on the adjacent bench with 170 francs (about £17) in it, which I took. Just enough to see me through…

When I got back to the dreadful *foyer* that evening, there was a brand new summer blazer lying on my bed and a pair of (almost) new light shoes underneath it. Both blazer and shoes were a perfect fit. I have no idea as to their provenance. Harbour would dismiss these 'coincidences', of course, but I find myself unable to do so. I wish he would exercise a bit of humility and produce another 140 pages on the lines of Why God (If He Exists) Invariably Answers Prayer. I shall fill the pool in readiness.

The Pain in Spain

I went to Spain for about 45 minutes. This is how it happened. I was on a tiny train in the Pyrenees between Pau and Oloron-Ste-Marie, the last place of any size before the Spanish frontier, when I met Corinne, 24, a beautiful French girl with legs to die for. These, however, were heavily bruised and I wondered, naughtily, if it was from love-making, but it turned out to be from riding: 'I always prefer to feel a horse *entre mes jambes*,' she told me.

Since this confidence was extended within five minutes of our meeting, I wasn't that surprised when she invited me to spend the night at her house in Oloron. Quite platonically, of course, since she had a Spanish boyfriend, Paulo, aged 30. I was a bit worried about this, since Spanish males are notoriously jealous and violent, but Paulo turned out to be a gentle charmer. He even arranged for his mother, who lived nearby and rejoiced in the name of Resurrection, to give me Spanish lessons.

Corinne and Paulo fed me a superb evening meal, fish *à l'espagnole* with onions and potatoes, and a very posh white wine. Next morning I felt tired, so left them a note saying that I had a touch of 'nervous gastritis' and would they mind if I stayed on a day or two to rest? The 'nervous gastritis' was a master stroke – one I have used before when scrounging – since it makes your hostess guiltily wonder if she has food-poisoned you. I stayed with them for some days and Corinne fed me on delicious tortillas (potato omelettes) and lightly grilled pork chops with rice until my stomach was magically better. My double bed was extremely comfortable too, so, taken all round, it was one of my best scrounges ever…

But all good things must come to an end, and eventually I had to move to an hotel while I went on with the (free) Spanish lessons. I stuck Corinne and Paulo with the hotel bill, too, which I reckon was one of the most despicable things I have ever done. The only thing to be said in my defence when I abuse hospitality thus is that I am aware I'm behaving like an arsehole. By now I had spent all the money I had saved for Spain, but decided to attempt the trip nevertheless.

The ride up through the Pyrenees (which I prefer to the Alps any day) was one of the most dramatically picturesque I have ever undertaken. My only companions were a couple of even more than usually inscrutable Japanese girls and a small, oldie, white-bearded Englishman, a retired schoolmaster, I guessed, who looked exactly like a garden gnome. (He was kind enough to describe my French as 'useful'. Useful? My French is absolutely brilliant!)

We arrived at Canfranc, seven kilometres into Spain, amidst the eternal snows. It was extremely cold up there, yet the sun shone brightly in contrast with France which was buried in raincloud. There was an enormous derelict, grass-overgrown station, about the size of Victoria and Waterloo combined, which might have been put up by Mussolini (wrong country, I know) or Franco in his heyday, but now only two trains a day run out of it down to Jaca, Huesca and Zaragoza. But it was a genuine monstrosity. The Garden Gnome clapped his little hands together at the sight of it.

There really wasn't an awful lot to do in Canfranc. I went in search of the village church, but it was modern – and locked. Basking in the sun on the steps was a long, poisonous snake which I kicked out of the way. This struck me as something that could only have happened to me in Spain. (I have never even seen a snake in France.)

I went to a little supermarket and stole a bar of milk chocolate and an apple, since I was starving. I would have 'jumped' one of the many hotels but they were all closed, which seemed a bit odd in the middle of summer. So I caught the bus back. In a few weeks, assuming I am not in the clutches of the gendarmes, who are showing an increasing interest in my movements (ten of them turned up to arrest me for an unpaid hotel bill in Pau – I had to stick Corinne and Paulo with it once again), I shall return to Spain to visit Jaca, Huesca and Zaragoza and will describe for your benefit the life of a criminal degenerate in these cities...

De'Ath of the Affair

My mother being German, my parents were much enamoured of the novels of Philip Gibbs, an ex-Fleet Street journalist who wrote about relationships between England and Germany in the years before and after the First World War. In his most famous book, *Blood Relations*, a young English bride, Audrey, goes to Germany to marry Paul, the scion of Bavarian aristocracy. Audrey naturally chums up with the family's English governess who, one night at dinner, while the German nobs are discussing the impending war with England, leans across to her and whispers: 'They hate us, my dear.'

These five little words have returned to me vividly and frequently these past few weeks because I have come to the conclusion that the French hate all English people and me in particular. And I hate them back, of course.

It is important to draw a distinction between France and the French here. On the *Oldie* Internet site, for instance, I find myself described as a 'Francophile'. If that means that I love France, fair enough. If it means that I love the French, then it is a lie.

Why do I hate the French? I hate them, firstly, because they are rude and unhelpful. Just the other day, in a Limoges post office, I needed to make a phone call. I asked the clerk if they had a telephone. 'No,' he said. In fact, there was one just outside the post office. 'Why didn't you tell me that?' I recriminated after making my call. 'Because you asked if there was one inside, not outside,' he replied coldly. The same day, I had to take a bus to the Gare des Bénédictins, the Limoges railway station. 'Does this bus stop at the station?' I asked the surly driver. 'No,' he said.

In fact, it stopped just 100 metres from the station. But he didn't want to tell me that.

Again the same day – by no means untypical of a day in this strange country – I went for a cup of tea in the library café. Pouring the hot water on to the expensive tea bag, the waitress scalded her arm very slightly. She screamed loudly. Eleven people came to her aid. I know this because I counted them: the proprietor, two under-managers, four other waitresses and four cooks. When the confusion had died down, it was me, of course, the unfortunate Englishman, who was roundly blamed for the incident for having the presumption to order tea at 4 pm, *l'heure de thé anglais*.

I am actually writing this piece in a typical French bar-restaurant. I have made the mistake of sitting at a corner table beneath a hat and coat stand. It is almost *midi*, the sacred hour of lunch. Greedy Frenchmen and women, anxious to get their huge snouts in the trough, keep crashing into me as they hang up their coats and hats. No one apologises. In an hour or so's time, at the end of their meal (the French don't believe life can be worth living without a good lunch), they will crash into me again as they pick up their coats. Again, no one will apologise.

Another reason that I hate the French is that they have fallen in love with America and all things American. They show endless third-rate US gangster films on their rotten television. My best friend here in Limoges happens to be a Californian. He is worshipped and grovelled to wherever he goes. (It is naturally assumed that he is a dollar millionaire, which he is not; in fact, he is poor.) I wonder how these naive French people would react if they had to go and live in California. I don't think they would like it very much.

The French have fallen in love with modern technology, too, but they have yet to learn how to master it. They have the TGV trains and the Minitel (a kind of computerised phone book) but really very little else they know how to operate. The Limoges library, for instance, has electronic doors which, at opening times, invariably get stuck. Someone has to come down and open them manually. French breakfast television is entirely taken up with demonstrating state-of-the-art electronic gadgets which no one could conceivably need or know how to work.

The French have a terrible reluctance to commit themselves to anything or anyone. When I telephone a *foyer* to ask if it might be possible to come and stay for a few days, the *directeur*'s response is invariably the same: '*Tout est possible.*' He doesn't want to commit himself, in other words. Nothing is easy in France. The dry-cleaning shop is never open when you expect it to be and the cathedral is always shut on a Sunday, the one day you might reasonably expect it to stay open…

Perhaps I am merely tired of France after ten years. I am certainly tired of being the one person in the whole country who doesn't smoke. You meet a beautiful girl, you get to know her a bit, you finally get to kiss her … and she reeks of tobacco smoke. Like all her fellow countrymen, she has no sense of humour and takes everything you say literally.

I am certainly tired of French bureaucracy (France is the most bureaucratic country in Europe) and of having to fill in forms in triplicate for the minutest transaction, like changing a few pounds sterling at the post office. (A morning can easily be spend doing this). Roll on the euro!

I think what I am actually saying is that I am fed up with France. Perhaps it is time to be coming home.

Dosshouse de Luxe

Returning to the university after an absence of 40 years is, to cite Anthony Powell, 'to drive a relatively deep fissure through variegated seams of Time'. I had gone back to Oxford to deposit 40 copies of *The Oldie*, which had become too heavy to carry around, in my old college library. I'm not sure that the faded blonde librarian who reluctantly accepted them wasn't the same woman who used to patronise me back in the late 1950s. If not, it was her sister. She certainly helped me to recapture – Powell again – all the crushing melancholy of the undergraduate condition…

My old college let me stay for seven nights without payment, which was pretty decent of them, but on the eighth, there was nothing for it but the horrible Oxford Night Shelter. Waiting down there with all my paltry worldly goods in a small suitcase (the shelter is situated in a very depressing part of the city, somewhere between the police station and the law courts), I couldn't help reflecting how low I have sunk since those halcyon student days. At a cocktail party I gave in my last summer term (1960), the first three guests to arrive were W H Auden, the Professor of Poetry, the entertainer Dudley Moore, now dying of a degenerative brain disease, and my old pal Ken Loach, who is still making worthy, if slightly boring, films with a socialist message. (For sheer name power, this was only exceeded by a Christmas champagne party in 1972 when my then wife and I entertained *à la* Jeffrey Archer the then Archbishop of Canterbury Michael Ramsey, the novelist Daphne du Maurier and our next-door neighbour who happened to be the First Sea Lord.)

I hit a particularly bad night at the Oxford shelter. I imagine all nights are bad there (it was a real culture shock after the superb French *foyers*), but this one was doubly so, since a pathetic cripple, with whom I had actually been talking over the foul meal three hours earlier, managed to die (of cirrhosis of the liver) in the only toilet soon after midnight. The place was suddenly alive with doctors, police and paramedics, so we weren't able to use the toilet. I don't suppose there is a single person reading this article who doesn't have access to a toilet, either at home or at work, 24 hours a day, and not to have that access (you are not allowed out of a shelter once it is closed for the night) is probably the most degrading and demeaning thing I have ever experienced, and that includes 'slop-out' at HMP Exeter in 1993.

I wasn't going to put up with any more of this kind of thing, so next morning, via 'paying' coach to London and 'jumping' train to Cambridge, I set out for 'the other place', where there is another night shelter, Jimmy's, which is supposed to be a cut above the Oxford one. It certainly couldn't turn out any worse...

Hmm. Not very prepossessing. The usual line of drunks, tramps, psychopaths and other derelicts waiting to descend the steps to the shabby basement of a Zion Baptist Church. The usual smell of mingling cheap tobacco, cannabis and stale urine. But who is this arriving? The Mayor of Cambridge, no less, wearing his chain of office, descending from his chauffeur-driven car, accompanied by the Lady Mayoress. (Jimmy's is his pet charity for the year 2001.) At least, if the Mayor is going to be present, the food should be OK tonight, said the cynical journalist of 40 years (myself). And so it proved: meat pie followed by the most delicious trifle. The Mayor and I got on like a house on fire. (My own great-grandfather was Mayor of Cambridge in 1874.)

But the food was good the following night as well: avocado with prawns, chicken curry, chocolate whip. And it was good the night after that and again the night after that... The fact is, I seem to have fallen on my feet again. Jimmy's is probably the best night shelter in Britain. It is run by a bunch of dedicated people, half of them Christian believers, half of them not, who really seem to care about their clients. I am a criminal degenerate, as I said in August, but I am not so sunk in corruption that I cannot recognise pure goodness when I meet it face to face. And the people who run Jimmy's, staff and volunteers, are really good people, make no mistake. I shall write more about them next month.

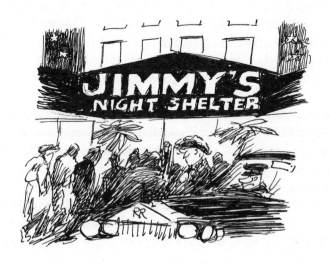

Down Among the Dead-beats

Any evening about 7 pm a motley crew of about 25 men and women, drunks, druggies, psychopaths and other assorted winos and tattooed weirdos may be seen descending the steep steps down to the basement of a Zion Baptist church on the far side of Parker's Piece in the unfashionable eastern suburb of Cambridge. These people, you may think, are the scum of the earth. They stink to high heaven, but they are descending into hell. They resemble the squirming insects you discover when you lift up a very large stone; they represent, if you like, the soft, rotten underbelly of Tony Blair's Britain.

For about a month, I shared a very small room at Jimmy's Night Shelter with Gary ('Stretch'), a zombie-like Frankenstein monster who screamed in his drunken nightmares and kept the rest of us awake; with Cockney Don, a small, pathetically raddled alcoholic who nightly abused and threatened me and finally challenged me to a duel (walking sticks at dawn on Parker's Piece); with Paul, a dreadful, broken-down Scottish drunk with surprisingly exalted literary tastes (he had already read the entire Booker short list); with Philip, a pleasant young Geordie who was looking for a proper job and decent accommodation – he was, perhaps, one of the ten per cent of Jimmy's clients who actually managed to improve their lot instead of sinking deeper and deeper into degradation. (Oddly enough, this statistic is precisely replicated across the Channel where I lived and slept 'rough' for ten years.)

All in all, these horrifying people gave a new dimension to the concept of 'Care in the Community', which is shorthand for nobody – except the Night Shelter – can be bothered to help them.

Jimmy's is named after an old tramp who died many years ago and is buried somewhere far away beneath a motorway bridge. It is managed by one Richard Howlett, a former BT middle manager, a curiously maternal figure, who never finds it in himself to criticise or condemn any of his disgusting guests. He and his wife Joan, an attractive but altogether more formidable character, founded Jimmy's five years ago and it is now the most notorious, in the best sense, night shelter in Britain. They are aided and abetted by a highly professional staff: Peter, Ken, Adam, Jane, Liz, Gwen and Rachel. To say that these workers are 'dedicated' would be an understatement. They display a tenacious efficiency and tact in dealing with their difficult charges which is unprecedented in my own (considerable) experience.

Jimmy's is considered 'a success' since it rids the streets of Cambridge, the proud, inward-looking university city, where so many sleep rough, of about 25 undesirables per night.

At 7.30 pm a delicious meal is served by voluntary workers. Last night it was tomato soup, chicken cooked in white wine with mushrooms, mashed potatoes, fresh green beans, and apple crumble, although a more typical menu might be prawn cocktail, roast pork with all the trimmings, fruit trifle. At any kind of decent restaurant in Cambridge, a very expensive place, you would pay £25 for a comparable repast, so I reckon I am eating at the rate of £175 a week.

What worries me a bit is the voluntary workers. They are another motley crew – retired people, pensioners, students, churchy 'do-gooders' – some of whom give the impression that they are doing it for themselves rather than to help anybody else. These people strike me as what the French punningly call *bénévoleurs*, i.e. they mean well, but they are, in fact, robbing you of your own space in search of their own self-fulfilment.

A month at Jimmy's raises in acute form the almost theological question of whether human life has any value *per se* and whether the pathetic forms lying drugged in front of the awful wall-to-wall 'soaps' on the telly have any future worth saving them for. Richard and Joan Howlett, being Christians, would presumably say that these people, however derelict, contain the divine spark and are worth helping and saving (from themselves). This is the central ethic of 'Jimmy's' and what, I suppose, makes it so successful in its own terms. It is certainly better than if it was being run on purely humanist or secular lines, as most other British night shelters are. But, I still have my doubts. Hitler's solution would have been to put these criminals, these parasites on society, in front of a firing squad. I'm not sure he wasn't right. (I would have been shot, too, of course.)

I write these words beside the dreaming waters of the River Cam. It is a fine morning in early autumn. A punt has just drifted by and a young woman asked, 'Is that a real person?' when she saw me! An interesting theological, existential question, reflecting one posed about me in the letters column of *Oldie* 150. Am I a real person? I shall try to answer this from my next destination, North Africa. Carnal contact with young Arab girls may help me to decide. Or even young Arab boys. Who knows?

154

Moany Christmas,
Everyone

One wouldn't expect an English provincial library, let alone a French one, to carry all the novels of Elizabeth Bowen (1899–1973) but the magnificent Médiathèque in Limoges has them, including her masterpiece and my personal favourite, *The Death of the Heart* (1938), which I have been reading over again during a very pleasant *été indien* in the library's *jardin d'hiver*. At one point, she writes perceptively about someone like me: 'The finer the nature, and the higher the level at which it seems to live, the lower, in grief, it not only sinks but dives; it goes to weep with beggars and mountebanks, for these make the shame of being unhappy less.'

Talk about hitting the nail on the head! This remark is so apposite that I am thinking of making it the text not merely of this piece but also of my autobiography, *Sorry, I'm Not in Service*.

Grief, for me, began 24 years ago on a gloomy November evening when I walked out on my wife and young children, then aged 13 and nine. Their little faces at the window are with me still. I didn't go at once to weep with beggars and mountebanks – that came later. (There are those, I know, who would say that I was then already a mountebank, which my BBC Dictionary defines as 'a person who tries to deceive people by claiming to be able to do wonderful things'.)

That evening, I walked down to the Finchley Road Tube station in a daze, without any clear idea of where I was going. When I got to the ticket office window, I heard myself saying 'Aldgate', because

I knew that somewhere down the Commercial Road was a group of Anglican monks and nuns, the Community of St Katharine, an offshoot of the Community of the Resurrection, who might be prepared to take me in.

The infamous De'Ath luck held even in these inauspicious circumstances because the nun who opened the spyhole in the Convent's wicket gate was 'nun' other than Sister Denzil, whom I happened to know and who also knew my wife. I told her what I had done and she allowed me to stay for one night in a very bare room, and the night turned into a long weekend and the weekend into several weeks – the shape of things to come. I vividly remember her, on that first night, mixing me a rich mug of Horlicks to help me to sleep, which it did. (Sister Denzil would often have to see off 'beggars and mountebanks', begging for food and shelter, from St Katharine's back door, and, a sensitive soul, she wept copiously when she did so.)

This way of life, i.e. still trying to maintain high ideals while living off the charity of others, continued for many years. In 1990, in keeping with what I still like to think of as my fine nature and still anxious to live at the highest level (I speak existentially, not materially), I decided to write a book about opera, which has always seemed to me the most sublime of all the arts – incorporating all the arts, in fact. The book was to be called *A Year in the Life of Opera North*. Opera North liked the idea, and it was agreed that I should live for a year, at their expense, at the Queen's Hotel in Leeds.

Unfortunately, when the time came to meet the bill, they were insolvent. My advance from André Deutsch, a notoriously mean publisher, went nowhere near to meeting it. So I was prosecuted and given an 18-month suspended sentence at Oxford Crown Court.

The descent to weep among beggars and mountebanks had begun, and I have to say that I feel it reached its nadir as recently as this past summer when a man in the bed next to mine died at the Oxford Night Shelter (see *Oldie* 151).

Ms Bowen is spot on when she suggests that what one is truly ashamed of in all this is not being materially poor but being unhappy. In fact, I have never been poor in my life. I have always been relatively rich or flat broke. Most of the time I have been flat broke.

I am flat broke as I write this. The only people who have ever given to me are other people who are also flat broke. If I have learned one thing from all of these years *à la misère* it is that it is the poor, not the rich, who give.

There must be a message there for this season, but I am not sure what it is. All I know is that I have been unhappy for many years and that I am unhappy now, but that I am trying to do something about it.

Confessions of De'Atheist

s we enter the New Year, I find my life dominated by five
As: Atheism, Anne, Avignon, Autobiography, Articles. I will
explain… Having spent my first 40 years in the embrace of
two further As, Anglicanism and Agnosticism, having then spent
20 years as a Roman Catholic and made an abortive attempt to
become Orthodox, I have finally decided that I am an Atheist. Man
invented God, not the other way round, because he finds the
thought of being alone in the Universe and of his own inevitable
extinction, personal and general, intolerable. So I now identify
more than ever with Larry, the protagonist of Somerset
Maugham's *The Razor's Edge*, a man of deeply religious instincts
and aspirations who cannot bring himself to believe in God.

Becoming an Atheist after 64 years living with God, or with the
idea of God, is a terrifying, deeply unsettling, vertiginous
experience. It leaves an enormous spiritual gap. I still go to Mass
every morning because I need 30 minutes of peace and quiet at the
beginning of each difficult day, but I have (almost) given up
praying. I also, bizarrely, retain some devotion to Mary, Our
Blessed Lady, but She probably only compensates for the absence
of a sexy, sympathetic female in my daily life.

That female ought to be Anne, 33, a beautiful Syrian girl with legs
and breasts to die for. I am deeply in love with Anne. Unfortunately,
her name in Arabic, Waafa, means fidelity. Even more unfortunately,
she is married to my best friend in France, Bernard, so this is going
to be a very long shot indeed. Bernard is 22 years older than Anne
and, like many Frenchmen of his generation, eats and drinks to
excess. I have to admit to wickedly encouraging him in this in the

hope that he will drop down dead one day, when Anne will fall into my lap like a ripe plum. This is a dreadful thing to confess and, were I still a believer, I would do so to God, but I have decided to confess to 40,000 *Oldie* readers instead, Of course, my fear is that, if Bernard does drop down dead, Anne will not fall into my lap but return to the bosom of her family in Syria instead. At least, being in love with her takes my mind (almost) off the other girls, so I am saving valuable time and sexual energy. There is no fool like an oldie fool, you will say, and you would be right...

Anne is studying French literature at the University of Avignon and, in order to be near her and to impress her with my amazing intellect, I am planning to move down there very soon. I have reservations about this move because Avignon, far from being the terrestrial paradise of most French people's imagination, is in fact a boring, provincial market town, posing as the cultural centre of the universe. It is, not to mince words, pretentious, the one thing I cannot abide. Moving down there will involve considerable sacrifice. It does have its plus points, however: excellent weather all the year round; the superb Visa *foyer* where one eats like a king; and Shakespeare, the best English bookshop in Europe, presided over by my dear oldie friend Wolfgang Zuckermann, 79.

In Avignon, I hope to go on writing my autobiography. It describes infancy (with a German mother in war-torn London); schooling; National Service in Germany; Oxford with Richard Ingrams (who he?); the BBC, where I was a producer at the age of 23, confirming the accuracy of Trollope's observation that success is a misfortune whenever it occurs but never more so than when it happens to someone young; marriage and children; a colourful sex life; travels all over the world, including a love/hate relationship with France and the French; descent into crime and punishment; a long spiritual journey, culminating in Atheism.

It will be, forgive me for saying so, a modern masterpiece, so please order your copy now!

Finally, I hope to go on writing for *The Oldie*. Articles number about 50 to date. Some readers, including one or two envious fellow journalists, have written accusing me of deliberately seeking out difficult, painful situations in order to gather material. I can only assure them that this is not the case. Anyone who intentionally spent time, as I have, in HMPs Dorchester, Exeter, Oxford and Winchester and aboard the 'floating' prison, HMP Weare, as well as at Cap Horn, the unspeakably disgusting *foyer* in Caen, would have to possess some kind of death wish, which I certainly don't. Other readers have suggested that in adopting this strange 'lifestyle', I am subconsciously trying to punish myself for past sins, chiefly those of neglect. There may be a grain of truth in that.

Back Where I Belong

I always thought that, sooner or later, I would be sent to prison in France. I had a secret dread of this because French prisons have a very bad reputation. Everything is bad about French prisons except the food. I was once walking past the little local prison in Tarbes in the Pyrenees and I saw trays of beautiful fruit and vegetables being carried in. 'I suppose this is for the officer's mess,' I said to the 'screw' on the gate. 'Not at all,' he assured me. 'This is for our lads…'

It was my own fault that I was sent to prison, although I had not (for once) committed any offence. I had merely exceeded my quota of 30 days at the *foyer* in Limoges and, not wishing to turn me out into the winter cold, they arranged an automatic transfer to the old prison in Brive, one hour south of Limoges. The prison is now being used as an emergency *foyer*, but it is still a prison, make no mistake…

I experienced that familiar sinking feeling in the pit of my stomach as I rang the bell at the iron gate and settled down for a long wait. Somehow I knew that whoever answered it would be a misshapen figure, a dead ringer for the late Marty Feldman, and so it proved. But, rather to my surprise, he (Jean-Luc) offered me a welcoming cup of coffee.

There are two things about Brive which make it hard to forget you are a prisoner, if only a voluntary one. The first is the omnipresence of bunches of dangling keys: keys to let you in the main gate; keys to the cell blocks; keys to the refectory; keys to the office; even keys to the linen cupboard and the toilets. The second is the stench, which is more than merely that of an old building

161

(Brive was a castle before it was even a prison). It is, like the keys, omnipresent and it is the ancient stench of human suffering.

My single cell was surprisingly comfortable. (I had asked for a single because I wanted to get some writing done.) Furniture consisted of no more than an extremely hard bed, a table, a chair and a washbasin, but it was well heated, and in three days I got an amazing amount of work done. I saw my fellow prisoners only at mealtimes – the food, as I had anticipated, was excellent – and, being mostly oldies, they had the good sense to leave me alone. I worked either in my cell or in the well-equipped library and I felt perfectly safe and happy. On the Monday morning, I was 'released' and Jean-Luc gave me his hideous claw to shake. It really hadn't been a bad experience at all.

By way of contrast, and to celebrate becoming an atheist, as described last month, and since the Limoges *foyer* was still full, I decided to make a 'spiritual' retreat (I'm not really religious, I've decided, I'm spiritual) at a convent near St-Léonard-de-Noblat, an ancient mediaeval city east of Limoges, high up in the Massif Central. The train deposits you in the middle of nowhere and I was somewhat at a loss. The only other descending passenger was a religious-looking lady, so I asked her if she happened to know the Centre Spirituel Jean XXIII. 'I ought to,' she replied. 'I'm the Mother Superior.' What a piece of luck! There are times when I really have to believe that the God in whom I no longer believe is still looking after me...

We were met by a chauffeur-driven car with another nun, Sr Monique, at the wheel and we shot off into the deep Limousin countryside. Sr Monique drove like the clappers – I've noticed this about nuns: they either drive like maniacs or they crawl down the middle of the road. So within a few hours of being released from prison in Brive, I found myself in another prison, a Roman Catholic one this time.

I was the only guest with five nuns: Sr Marie-Françoise, the

Mother Superior; Sr Marie-Hélène, an attractive, 'worldly' nun; Sr Généviève, an intellectual; Sr Françoise, an eccentric, and Sr Monique, the community workhorse. They looked after and fed me well enough, but I couldn't help feeling rather confined by the Catholic ritual: compulsory Matins and Vespers and daily Mass in the nearby town. I didn't dare tell the nuns I had recently become an atheist. To tell the truth, I felt more confined locked up with them than I had done in Brive. That had had all the advantages of a prison sentence without the drawbacks. The chief advantage, of course, is that nobody from the outside world can get at you. '*L'enfer, C'est les autres,*' said Sartre. Hell is other people.

The End is Nigh

Will the Circle be Unbroken?
Conversations About Death
BY STUDS TERKEL

It is a number of years since I first reviewed a Studs Terkel book. That was for the old *Punch* when Alan Coren was only the literary editor. Terkel was 48. I observed then, as I observe now, that he is brilliant at getting people talking on a given subject but lousy at getting them to shut up. Although he pays fulsome tribute here to his editor of 35 years, André Schiffrin, he could have done with a much tougher one.

The book is 400 pages long but the truly insightful remarks about death, its alleged subject, could have been contained in just four. I suppose it is a bit much to expect Terkel, now 88, to move around a great deal, but one does get fed up with the views of his native Chicago. Why couldn't he, given the importance of his subject, have spread his net a bit wider? The trouble with Chicagoans is that, beneath their tough-guy stance, they are revoltingly sentimental in the worst American way.

Now for those insights. The central one, which occurs over and over, among believers and non-believers alike, is that there is no such thing as Heaven and Hell. Heaven and Hell are here and now. I go along with that. If this review reaches Richard Ingrams safely from my hidey-hole in France and he prints it and sends me, say, £75, then I am in Heaven. If it fails to reach him or if he fails to print it and send my £75, then I am in Hell. It's as simple as that.

We are all on death row, of course, as an African-American who was actually on it for two years, sent there by an all-white jury for a rape and murder he didn't commit – gently points out. And the film director Haskell Wexler observes something else I've noticed, that with the ageing process, with death looming, it becomes harder and harder to sort out priorities: 'With my growing awareness of death, I have a completely different feeling of time. I have more immediate priorities. In past years, I would say, "Well, so I'll wait around for a couple of weeks…" Now, I'm impatient with things I want to do. Usually it centers down into relations with people, to human things. It's very hard to do when you're on the track the way I've been: to write this article, to make this little film, to make all those others. Wait a minute. What's more important? Awareness of death may be liberating for some people, but it makes me a little more tense.'

Terkel has a weakness for celebrities – the writer Kurt Vonnegut, the blind folk singer Doc Watson, the actress Ute Hagen are all involved here – but they don't really have much to say, although Ms Hagen gives a neat answer to the question of what, if anything, comes after: 'I think it's over, period. It's the end. But I do believe … that there is something in the spirit surviving and being near and being around. I also think that nobody is really dead until nobody remembers you anymore.'

The most succinct summary comes from Hank Oettinger, a retired printer: 'Afterlife does not exist. It is not necessary. Life goes on on Earth, and we have our memories. The only life that is necessary is the one that we're enjoying now.'

The quote I personally most identified with was from Kia Pharoah, a 'collector' (of debts and protection money), a professional criminal, in fact: 'It's a terrible thing for a man to go out a complete failure. The one sin of nature is that we grow old and die. The great gift of life we got is that they gave us that gift to be a fucking failure … Now, I don't fear dying. The great fear I have is dying a failure… We all go. I don't want to go out a nothing. I want to go out a man among men.'

Off the Rails

Napoleon said that England was a nation of shopkeepers. The French, who will believe anything, still believe this, and they also believe that we are a nation of pederasts. In both cases, I'm afraid, it's a case of the pot calling the kettle black because no people are more commercially minded than the money-grabbing French and in no other country have I been so persistently bothered by homosexuals.

The *petit commerçants* have now had a field day with the arrival of the euro in January (all their prices have gone up, of course) and the final disappearance of the franc on 17 February. It is the most exciting thing that has happened to the greedy French shopkeepers in their lifetimes; in fact, it is probably the most exciting thing that has happened since Corporal Bonaparte made his wildly inaccurate observation.

Euro Day in Avignon, where I now live when I'm in France, dawns cold and clear. As I cross the Rhône over Pont Edouard Daladier at 7.30 am, the sky is already blue/black over the city, heralding longer and finer days to come. The Palais des Papes and the Cathedral, surmounted by Our Lady clad in gold leaf, are bathed in a pink, ethereal light. Avignon is spread out before me like the Heavenly Jerusalem. With the onset of the euro, it feels as if a new era is beginning.

To celebrate it, I head for a more up-market café than usual, Le Parisien in Place Pie. I want to see how they are coping with the new currency. I am just in time to hear the rather disagreeable Madame (a classic money-grabber) instructing the charming young waiter, Jeffrois, to give her customers their change in euros.

A worried frown appears on Jeffrois's handsome brow. I proffer him a 50-franc note for my coffee and his frown deepens.

Finally, *le pauvre* Jeffrois is obliged to go to the bank across the square to work out how much he owes in euros. In his confusion, he forgets to pick up my 50 francs. It is barely 8 am on Euro Day and already I am nearly 100 francs ahead of the game! I continue to profit in this way for several days while the French, whose brains tend to be on the small size, mop their brows in perplexity. Serves them right! The euro may be a great success at the international level but in the cafés and restaurants of provincial cities like Avignon it is total chaos from the word go. And yours truly is exploiting it, of course…

However, I am soon punished for my avarice and dishonesty. I leave my jacket unattended over a chair for two minutes at Visa *foyer* while returning my plate to the serving hatch and someone unbuttons an inside pocket and removes my EC passport. I am not secure enough to live in France without a passport, which one is called upon to produce almost daily, so I decide to come back to England.

The first bed-and-breakfast place in Cambridge, whither I return after the usual nightmare journey, charges me £40 for one night. I could live for several weeks in France for that! Then I am lucky enough to discover Sleeperz Hotel, where a room can be had for as little as £25. I have fallen on my feet again.

Sleeperz, situated right by Cambridge railway station, is a new concept in hotels. It is based on the premise that since you are on a journey you may as well maintain the illusion that you are still travelling. Long, train-like corridors are split into tiny cabins or couchettes with the most comfortable bunk beds I have ever slept in. There is even room for a tiny en-suite bathroom with shower and toilet. It is a bit like being on the Orient Express – you expect to see the landscape of Transylvania drifting by. In fact, all you get to see is dreary old Cambridge. You expect (and hope) to find an exotic student wondering if the hotel will accept euros…

But it is a fun hotel to live in. Ham and cheese are served for breakfast along with warm croissants and good coffee and orange juice. So the Continental ambience is maintained. It is my deepest philosophical conviction that our remote ancestors never settled in one place but forever kept on the move in search of fresh pasture for their cattle. Restlessness is bred deep within us. A few weeks at Sleeperz suits my peripatetic lifestyle to perfection. (Other branches are to open soon in Bath and York, so if you find yourself near those cities, do give Sleeperz a try.)

Anyway, a few weeks here has taken the edge off the culture shock of returning to the country of the non-running trains. Sleeperz is precisely that: a permanently non-running train, and therefore deeply symbolic of contemporary Britain. Its kindly proprietor, Barrie Munn, even writes 'It is a pleasure to be of service to you' on his invoices. For once, it sounds sincere.

Sleeperz Hotel is at Station Road, Cambridge, CB1 2TZ.

Wanted: Virgin Berth

I am sitting in the Nip In, a small café/library on Cambridge's unfashionable Mill Road, trying to make a single cup of tea last for two hours. Having been thrown out of Sleeperz Hotel for not paying the bill, I am facing the prospect of life on the streets again. Outside, a malignant chemical spring rain is falling, turning Mill Road into a miasma of misery. It is impossible to imagine a more depressing scene. I am beginning to understand why, Christmas apart, early spring is the peak season for suicides. Depressed people emerging from the long English winter cannot handle the return of the sun, of strength and vitality… Neither can I.

On the other side of the street, someone I vaguely recognise is hurrying through the rain. It is Rachel, one of the assistants at Jimmy's Night Shelter, known in my private notation as OCW (Over-Conscientious Woman) bordering on BC (Bossy Cow). However, I am relieved to see her. I streak across Mill Road, dodging the traffic, to ask if there are any free places at Jimmy's. She says, non-committally, that there may be. If I care to come along at six, I will only have to stand for an hour in the freezing rain to find out.

So at 6 pm here we are again, waiting with the drunks, the weirdos, the outcasts of the earth. Sammy, the little Irish drunk, still lurches against me at every opportunity; Paul, the big Scottish drunk, still puts his arms round my shoulders and declares me 'a fine figure of a man', proving that he is not without insight; Don, the raddled Cockney drunk, continues to heap abuse and curses on me.

Finally, at 7 pm, I am admitted for supper in a soaking wet state, since I possess no overcoat. There would seem to have been a bit of a slash in the food budget: unappetising vegetable soup, soggy ham fritters with chips and baked beans. Not quite up to the high cuisine of last autumn when I feasted with the Mayor and Mayoress (Jimmy's was his pet charity for 2001). But it is still better than the streets. The De'Ath luck has held.

I manage a few hours' sleep on the top bunk with my old friend Archie, an ex-convict Magwich lookalike, one of Jimmy's regulars, snoring peacefully beneath me. But I am overcome with humiliation at having had to return to Jimmy's in the first place. After a few nights there, I am haunted by one question and one question only: how to escape.

The De'Ath luck holds again. At the arts cinema I attend daily – the only place in Cambridge where they leave you alone when you don't buy a drink – there is a pretty girl named Philippa in charge of the box office who happens to mention that her parents run an upmarket bed-and-breakfast, Waterside, in nearby Ely. I check in there for a few days and it is as though I have gone from the hostel from hell to the hotel from heaven…

Waterside is steeped in history, having been a brickmaker's house in the 18th century; a grocer and tea merchant's house and shop in the 19th century; and then for some 30 years a home for unmarried mothers! For the last five years, it has been in the hands of Jane and Norman Latimer, who run the best bed-and-breakfast (and tea rooms) in East Anglia. And I should know because I have stayed in all of them. Sometimes I have even paid the bill.

Jane Latimer somehow manages to achieve a high level of luxury and comfort but not so high as to make you yourself feel uncomfortable. Apart from the usual features like cable TV, radio, hairdryer etc, there are wall-to-wall good books (essential in my case) and a hospitality tray of exotic teas and Horlicks, which guarantees a good night's sleep, as they used to say in the adverts of my youth. The most luxurious item of all is a fluffy white housecoat (for use in the en-suite bathroom) in which I lounge around all day feeling like an Eastern potentate or pasha instead of a bum off the streets. It is all extremely therapeutic.

Biggest treat of all: over breakfast of smoked salmon and scrambled eggs you look out on the shining Great Ouse river and the Ely marina, where the Cambridge Girls' Eight practise for their annual run every morning. Most of them are deadly butch, needless to say, but there is the odd pretty one for me to lust after which gives me the feeling that, even in this silent spring, there is still some hope around the corner...

At Waterside, I feel I have died and gone to heaven. The Latimers have mastered the difficult art of leaving their guests alone to enjoy their privacy. Unfortunately, Waterside is on the market and the Latimers are off to Scotland to pursue perfectionism in a small hotel not far from Fort William. I am seriously thinking of following them up there.

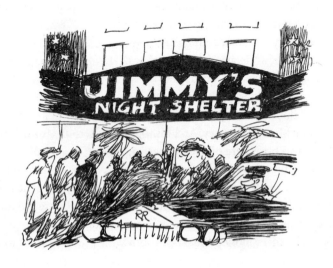

The Secret of Room 2

It is November 1914 during the early, dark, dreadful days of the First World War. A ten-year-old boy named Michael emerges from the front door of No 71 Chesterton Road, Cambridge, clutching the hand of his older brother, Frank. In his other hand he holds an old-fashioned leather football. The two boys cross the footbridge over the River Cam, and make their way on to Jesus Green. From there, they process to Midsummer Common where they give their ball a good kicking...

A few years later, Frank Ramsey, a brilliant young man in whom all his family's hopes and expectations resided, will be dead at 16. Forty-seven years later, in 1961, his younger brother, Arthur Michael Ramsey, who was carrying the football on that November day, will be made Archbishop of Canterbury. Ten years after that, he will offer the job as his press secretary to none other than yours truly. Thirty years later, yours truly, finding himself at a loose end in Cambridge while awaiting the renewal of his EC passport, will arrive at 71 Chesterton Road, now called Aaron House, in search of bed-and-breakfast accommodation. A plaque on the wall beside the front door says simply:

'Arthur Michael Ramsey, Archbishop of Canterbury from 1961 to 1974, was born here on November 14, 1904.'

When I first stayed at Aaron House in February of this year, I was given a small room on the second floor. It was pleasant and comfortable enough, but it did not speak Michael Ramsey to me. I caught just a whiff of him, however, next morning in the delightful, old-fashioned breakfast room which looks out on to a pleasant balcony and garden with the brutal modem edifice of the Cambridge DHSS and Job Centre looming in the distance.

I returned to Aaron House in early March and was given Room 3, a part of the much larger room on the first floor in which Michael Ramsey was actually born. In this room, his spirit was (and is) quite overwhelmingly present. During three nights there, he returned to haunt my dreams and to reprove me, in the most tender, compassionate and understanding way imaginable, for my new-found atheism. I soon saw that it was going to be difficult to remain an atheist in these circumstances.

On Sunday, 10 March, I returned to Aaron House yet again and was given their only en-suite, Room 2, which consists of the rest of the room in which Michael Ramsey was born. This large, sunny room, overlooking the Cam and Jesus Green, is perhaps the most agreeable bed-and-breakfast room I have ever stayed in, and I speak as one with experience of hotels and guest houses in many countries and continents. If I could afford to do so (it costs £45 a night), I would live in Room 2, Aaron House, in Cambridge, for ever. It, too, is imbued with Michael Ramsey's spirit, and that is one big spirit to be imbued with.

I go back a long way with Michael Ramsey. When I was just 16 and at school in North London, our housemaster, who was a bit of a shirt-lifter, used to take his favourite sixth-formers on Easter holidays to the Lake District. Who should be staying at our hotel in 1953 but Michael Ramsey, then Bishop of Durham, shortly to become Archbishop of York? I got to know him a bit then, but, 20 years later, when I became his press secretary, I got to know him a whole lot better.

Michael Ramsey was an eccentric and an egocentric, but that did not prevent him from being a great man. In fact, my friendship with him has led me to ponder deeply on the nature of greatness. What makes a great man? Two others universally acknowledged to be great, Winston Churchill and Charles de Gaulle, were also highly eccentric as well as egocentric. Yet two others whom I have had the pleasure of knowing personally, Malcolm Muggeridge and Terry Waite, also possessed these qualities in abundance.

I am writing these words in Room 7 at Aaron House on the second floor, where I have been banished because Rooms 2 and 3 are currently occupied. It is almost a relief to have escaped Ramsey's enormous, overwhelming spiritual presence. What he is saying to me, I know, is:

'Come off it, Wilfred, you're not really an atheist. You're only pretending to be one because you cannot face up to the challenge of the living God…'

There is much food for thought here. When I became Roman Catholic in 1979, Michael Ramsey wrote me a very nice letter from his retirement home in Durham. He said he sympathised with my conversion and was inclined to follow me but felt that, given his position, he couldn't. I now wish I had kept that letter. I would throw it back in his face and ask him to leave me alone.

No Rest for the Wicked

Jimmy's Night Shelter being full, I am on the streets at last. So I have finally gone to the dogs and, as George Orwell observed, the dogs really aren't that bad. The Cambridge nights are mild and I deal with the problem not by sleeping on a park bench but by taking a series of vigorous walks around the city. I now know Cambridge like the back of my hand.

Funny things keep happening. Two ravishing girls, aged about 14, stop me at 1 am and offer sex in exchange for the price of a hot dog. I am severely tempted but, not having any money, am obliged to move on; Shortly afterwards a police car draws up and I am ready to give myself up on a vagrancy charge, but it is only the Northants police shamefacedly asking the way to the Cambridge police station. I give them rather pompous directions ('Cross Parker's Piece and you'll find it lit up like a Christmas tree'), to which they respond humbly enough: 'Thanks for your time, squire.' I wonder what they'd say if they knew they'd just missed the chance to arrest an internationally wanted criminal and fugitive...

Some money falls in and, instead of returning to Jimmy's, I decide to take a short break in deepest Norfolk. At Walsingham, England's Nazareth, I come upon a bed-and-breakfast, Pilgrim's Rest, that I have never 'done' before. It is run by one Wendy Howse. There is something 'about' Wendy. I am not surprised to find a notice in the TV room proclaiming her to be a 'healer'. Nor am I very surprised when she invites me to join her at a 'healing' service at a spiritualist church out on the coast at Sheringham.

We set out on a fine spring evening. I have never been to a spiritualist church before and am suspicious of what they may get up to. Twenty or 30 local souls sit around the edges of a large basement room. The ambience of simplicity and sincerity is undeniable. In the centre of the room are four or five 'healers' who each spend 20 minutes or so massaging their clients in a strictly non-erotic way. I pick out, not entirely at random, a rather exotic divorcee named Tania whose massages border on the erotic but never actually crosses the line. At the end of the service, she makes a point of coming up to say that I will soon begin to feel very tired. Boy, she isn't kidding! I almost fall asleep on Wendy's shoulder on the way home. That night, I fall into a deep sleep and dream about my mother for the first time since 1988, when she died. All very rum. Next morning, I sleep late and miss Wendy's excellent breakfast…

I return to Cambridge and the life of the streets. In some ways it is a relief not to have to return to Jimmy's, where there are nightly fights between three Irishmen, Paddy, John and Sammy, which make eating supper a hazardous business. I guess the Irish just enjoy fighting.

Some more money falls in and I set off for a weekend in Aldeburgh on the Suffolk coast where, in my heyday, I owned a beautiful flat on the sea front. On the train to Saxmundham, I run into an old friend, George Melly, on his way to stay with the painter Maggi Hambling, whose portrait of George hangs in the National Portrait Gallery. I go back a long way with Good Time George: to 1959 when we danced the night away at the Anarchists Ball at the Fulham Town Hall; to a few years later when I interviewed him for the *Today* programme when he was writing *Flook* with Wally Fawkes for the *Daily Mail*; to this year's *Oldie* lunch. George is 75, a bit blind and a bit deaf. I ask him if there are any advantages to being old and he says he cannot think of a single one. But he is a kind enough to say that he likes my articles…

Aldeburgh has scarcely changed after 25 years – just a little more commercial activity, perhaps, and no Ben Britten, no Peter

Pears, no Laurens van der Post. Nor has the claustrophobically quiet holiday village of Thorpeness, two miles to the north, where I go for a row on the lake and get flung out of the local inn, the Dolphin, for not paying the bill.

I return to Cambridge to find a letter from my old nurse, Doris, who saved my life in 1949 when I went down with peritonitis at the age of 12. She has read my stuff in *The Oldie*, is now living near Cambridge, and would like to meet up. Doris is 77, her husband John, a neurophysiologist, is 80, but they are both so full of energy that they put me, a mere 65 this month, to shame. They take me out for lunch and back to their beautiful home in the nearby village of Harston, and just for a moment I experience a twinge of nostalgia for the bourgeois life I have rejected and left behind.

For what did you save my life 53 years ago, Doris? That I might walk the Cambridge streets? There has to be more to it than that.

Too Close for Comfort

Tucked away at the back of Jimmy's Night Shelter is a tiny room known as the 'Women's Room'. It is, or used to be, where female vagrants were accommodated. And a pretty disgusting bunch they were. Times, however, have changed. Jimmy's no longer accepts women, and their little room has been designated 'Room 5' for men while another of the men's rooms is being 'refurbished'. There is just room for six bunk beds in the small, foetid space. I spent a night in there recently, sleeping with five other unfortunates, and I wish to tell you exactly what it was like…

I retire to bed at 8.30 or so, after the meagre supper, in the hope of snatching an hour or two's rest before the others arrive. The first to do so is Duane, a thin, young, blond *Big Issue* seller. Duane is an extremely clean young man, which is just as well, since in Room 5 he isn't going to stay that way for long. He showers at what seems like hourly intervals, spends ages obsessively arranging and rearranging his clothes, sprays his pillow and duvet with air-freshener and – like me – feels strongly about admitting fresh air. Since we have only one tiny window between the six of us, this is going to be an uphill task.

I watch Duane, his prolonged ablutions at an end, slipping his pale, slender body beneath the duvet. It occurs to me, not for the first time, that I may be turning homosexual at the age of 65 after a lifetime of fancying only women. Not that I want to touch Duane or anything like that… I wonder how Duane would react? Go off and take another shower, probably.

The next resident to arrive is Paul, in the bunk adjacent to mine – there are about 18 inches between us; we must be breaching every Health and Safety regulation ever devised, but Richard Howlett, Jimmy's extremely compassionate manager, doesn't seem to care. Paul is a drunk, charming when sober, vicious when not. He has spent long periods in prison for drink-driving offences. There is something decidedly 'queer', in both senses, about him, too, and I fear for my anal virginity in the long night ahead. Really, what is coming over me?

A long wait – until past midnight – when Sammy, the little Irish drunk, who is incontinent as well as extremely smelly, is escorted in by the night shelter staff because he cannot walk unaided. They kiss him lovingly (not ironically) goodnight and it seems to me that you really need to be broken-down, alcoholic scum before you can expect any attention in a place like this. The fact has to be faced: the staff really only like down-and-outs; they can't be bothered with upright, clean-living (relatively), temporarily homeless, good citizens like myself. (Sammy threw a full bottle of expensive sherry at me in the street the other day. I grassed him up, of course, but what is the point when they aren't going to do anything?)

They love Sammy as much as I loathe him. They love people they can look down on and patronise and they hate people like me because they can't work out what I am doing there in the first place.

The bunk above Paul's is suddenly occupied, at 12.30 am, by somebody I have never seen before; a Rasputin look-a-like. I know nothing about him, but he looks a nasty piece of work...

Last to arrive, about 1 am, is Keith, a crippled, alcoholic beggar, not recently acquainted with soap and water, who clambers on to the bunk above mine. Keith is the resident I hate most of all. He throws his metal crutches to the ground with a great clatter, kicks me in the face as he climbs up, and proceeds to heap foul-mouthed abuse on me when I complain. I hope he dies during the night.

There are now six of us tossing and turning, snoring and farting, in a room about the size of a telephone booth. The air is soon foetid with our farts and the aroma of unwashed bodies and clothes. By 2 am I can stand it no longer and retreat to the day room to complain to Rachel (OCW: Over-Conscientious Woman; BC: Bossy Cow; BM?: Bucking for Management?), the assistant on night duty. But she is already asleep on a couch, or so it seems, and I don't want to disturb her. So I complain to Kenny, another insomniac resident, and I do not mince my words...

Kenny is sympathetic, but around 3 am I return to the fray. I finally manage three fitful hours and wake up at 6 am with a bad taste in my mouth, a foul stench in my nostrils, and my lungs full of polluted air. I return to the day room. Rachel, it transpires, was not asleep last night and overheard every colourful word of my complaint. So I am reprimanded, which seems unfair. But, at least, morning has risen and another hellish night is over. How long, O Lord, how long?

Home at Last

When I disembarked from the prison ship HMP Weare in 1998, the chaplain, the Rev Bill Browne-Cave, told me: 'If you can't settle in Cambridge, you can't settle anywhere.' Well, I have tried to follow his advice over these four years, but I have consistently failed. Cambridge struck me – still, in fact, strikes me – as an impossible place, with nothing to choose between the snobbish, inward-looking, self-regarding university, which it's impossible to penetrate, even if one wanted to, which I don't, and the bums off the street who inhabit Jimmy's Night Shelter.

Things, however, came to a head for me last May when, approaching the magic age of 65, I was forced to go in search of 'sheltered accommodation' for OAPs. Jimmy's being full, I had already passed several nights on the Cambridge streets – fortunately, it being summer, the nights were balmy as well as short – but I lost my nerve when a doctor told me I had suspected prostate cancer as well as extremely severe diabetes: 'If you don't get a roof over your head, you'll be dead in six months,' he said.

There is nothing like a death sentence and the prospect of extinction to galvanise one into action. I threw myself on the mercy of a very nice, efficient woman, Joan Howlett, one of the managers of Jimmy's, and within a few days she had found me a small 'studio' flat owned by a humanist housing association. What irony! To think that after all these years in the Christian Church (which never did anything to help me) I should end up with a bunch of non-believers.

The flat is in a large, purpose-built building in a remote suburb of Cambridge, and it actually looks more like an old folks' home than an apartment block. It is overheated and there is that dreadful odour of incontinent oldies mingling with disinfectant that is the hallmark of such places the world over. ('Cambridge's only above-the-ground cemetery,' I quipped to myself on my first morning.) But some of the old folks are quite sprightly and the place is supervised by an extremely attractive, sexy young blonde, Toni, self-obsessed in the nicest possible way, with whom I have fallen deeply in lust. For our Jubilee party in June, I went as Prince Charles and Toni came as the late Diana. That was a reunion to die for, I can tell you, with some very interesting body language (and contact) taking place behind our respective masks. (One old lady was kind enough to say that I was better-looking without the mask!) That is as much as I can tell you for now, since this is supposed to be a family magazine... There is no fool like an oldie fool, as I've remarked before.

The flat is really extremely pleasant – I've turned it into a kind of shrine to this publication by decorating it with more than 50 *Oldie* covers, and I can see myself living out the rest of my life in this place. Or so I thought until my brand-new, shiny EC passport arrived and with it a bad case of wanderlust to take its place alongside my lust for the scheme adviser. Italy this autumn, perhaps, with stop-offs to see my friends in Limoges and Avignon. I'm too young to stop still...

This is the first settled 'house' I've had in 25 years, since I left my wife and children in 1977 and began my wandering lifestyle. It is a very strange, unfamiliar feeling having somewhere to go back to in the evenings, something my children have been pressing me to do for many years now. I have, I admit, enjoyed decorating the place, getting hold of furniture (Joan and Richard Howlett have been absolute bricks), even waiting around for plumbers, electricians, etc. Moving is normally an extremely stressful experience – I have moved house about 300 times in my life – but this time I haven't found it so.

All this is too good to last, of course. I know in my heart of hearts that I shall soon be ready to take on Europe again. In fact, I shall probably be there by the time you read this. But I shall keep the flat on as a base. The final irony that I am now beholden to people who don't believe in God or the Church has not escaped me. The fact is that the humanists have done more for me in 50 days than the Christian Church has done in 50 years. Is there a message there? Is the God I no longer believe in trying to tell me something?

THE VIRGIN IN ENGLAND